# Book Production

The digital revolution has brought with it a wider range of options for creating and producing print on paper products than ever seen before. With the growing demand for skills and knowledge with which to exploit the potential of digital technology comes the need for a comprehensive book that not only makes it possible for production staff, editors and designers to understand how the technology affects the industry they work in, but also provides them with the skills and competencies they need to work in it smartly and effectively. This book is designed to satisfy this need.

*Book Production* falls into two parts.

- The first part deals with the increasingly important role of production as project managers, a role which has not been adequately written about in any of the recent literature on publishing.
- The second part deals with the processes and raw materials used in developing and manufacturing print on paper products. Case studies are used to illustrate why and how some processes or raw materials may or may not be appropriate for a particular job.

With expert opinions and case studies, and a consideration of the practices and issues involved, this new book offers a comprehensive overview of book production for anyone working, or training to work in or in conjunction with the book industry.

**Adrian Bullock** has for the past twenty years been Principal Lecturer on the undergraduate and postgraduate publishing programmes at Oxford Brookes University, UK, where he specialises in project and production management. He now runs Oxford Publishing Consultancy, which specialises in publishing project and production management, and allows him to put to practical use many of the techniques he spends his time teaching. He is also involved in extensive publishing consultancy work in the developing world, particularly in educational publishing, for bilateral and multilateral agencies such as the World Bank, the Asian Development Bank, the Soros Foundation, DfID, USAID, UNICEF and UNESCO.

# Book Production

Adrian Bullock

With a foreword by John Peacock

Routledge
Taylor & Francis Group

LONDON AND NEW YORK

KH

First published 2012
by Routledge
2 Park Square, Milton Park, Abingdon, Oxon OX14 4RN

Simultaneously published in the USA and Canada
by Routledge
711 Third Avenue, New York, NY 10017

*Routledge is an imprint of the Taylor & Francis Group, an informa business*

*British Library Cataloguing in Publication Data*
A catalogue record for this book is available from the British Library

*Library of Congress Cataloging in Publication Data*
Includes bibliographical references and index.
1. Publishers and publishing. 2. Book industries and trade. 3. Publishers
and publishing–Great Britain. 4. Book industries and trade–Great Britain.
5. Publishers and publishing–Technological innovations. 6. Book industries
and trade–Technological innovations. 7. Production management.
8. Project management. I. Title.
Z278.B93 2012
070.5–dc23
2011050219

ISBN: 978-0-415-59379-3 (hbk)
ISBN: 978-0-415-59380-9 (pbk)
ISBN: 978-0-203-14635-4 (ebk)

Typeset in Sabon
by Taylor & Francis Books

Printed and bound in Great Britain by the MPG Books Group

11/12/13

# Contents

# List of figures and tables

## Figures

## Tables

# Acknowledgements

I could not have written this book without the enormous amount of help I have received from a great many people in the industry – publishing as well as printing. It would be difficult to thank you all because there are so many of you and I am sure to miss someone out who should have been thanked. So, rather than risk doing that, I would like to say 'thank you' to you all. I know who you are, and you know too!

Finally, as usual, it is often the people least involved in the subject who get the most embroiled, listening patiently to stuff that makes little or no sense to them, and offering constructive criticism. So, my thanks and gratitude go to my immediate family: Berne, Hannah and Lizzie. My father and mother, Alan and Nibby, now sadly no longer alive, were both writers, and will understand why I dedicate this book to their memory.

# Foreword

When Adrian asked me to write a few words to introduce *Book Production* I was delighted to do so for a number of reasons.

First – because in today's mixed-media scene, any new book dedicated to book production is a valuable corrective and a timely one.

Publishing, as we all know, is simply in the business of communicating with readers in whatever form those readers wish to receive their product. Publishers, or at least the resourceful and receptive ones, listen carefully to readers' wishes, accept them willingly and respond to them. Digital products are a vital part of that response. Newer by far than print, digital products continue to make many more headlines than print – the successes of digital readers and tablets make good stories and sell devices.

But standing at the bedrock of nearly all forms of publishing is this basic truth, inconvenient as it may be: print at today's date continues to dominate publishing in all but specialist science and similar niche markets, and is unlikely to go away any time soon. So a first key message underlying *Book Production* is that books and book-making are *important* and *enduring* – culturally, socially, commercially.

Second – because I believe that to be involved in the making of books is an absorbing and demanding career choice which requires large doses of clear thinking, leadership and diplomacy in working with colleagues – but also requires larger than normal doses of solid and factual technical expertise. So it's vital that resources are available from which that expertise can be acquired, and that those resources are bang up to date, wide-ranging, practical in bent and concisely described.

No one needs reminding how quickly the technical aspects of digital and book delivery can change, how quickly styles and product lines can mutate, and how vital it is to continue understanding and delivering what works for customers, be it in terms of visual design, in product handling, in price and in value for money.

No one plays a more active part in these respects than the production specialist, whose range might extend from choosing typography and page design at one end, through the selection of paper, to an appropriate binding style – in effect deciding the whole look and fitness for purpose of the book, as well as its timely delivery. These are critical factors in any title's success or failure, and important responsibilities. This book will provide a vital 'tool-kit' for carrying out those responsibilities – understanding how to specify with confidence, how to control the passage of a book through your own company and externally, and how to understand, empathise and help resolve the challenges which your suppliers meet in fulfilling your work.

Third – because any book which can provide a lively and attractive overview of its subject for a non-specialist, as well as detailed knowledge and technical intricacies for the specialist, immediately serves a double function. I believe it's a strength of this book that it can be approached to great advantage by anyone in the publishing business, whether editors, designers, marketeers, sales people or accountants, and so can make a valuable contribution to the publishing business more widely.

So I would urge my fellow-colleagues involved in the specialism of book production to let your other publishing colleagues know about this book and recommend it to them.

Lastly – it's a pleasure to commend Adrian on bringing this excellent book successfully to publication. The contents distil a lifetime's experience in and commitment to the business of producing books, both as an international practitioner and as an academic and post-graduate tutor. I'm confident *Book Production* will take its place among the 'standard reads' on the subject, and that given the inexorable pace of technical and commercial change, this will be just the first in a series of new editions in the years to come.

John Peacock
April 2012

# Introduction

Project and production management is a key activity in any publishing context; whether it is dealing with printed books or digital products, their creation and development need to be planned and organised before they can appear in their final form. *Book Production* has been written for people working in or dealing with production at the start of the twenty-first century, in which traditional workflows, job descriptions, roles and hierarchies have been eroded and blurred, and where editors find themselves dealing with production issues and production with editorial ones. It has also been written for people who do not normally work in production, or who have no experience of publishing at all, who want to produce a book, but have no idea of where or how to start.

*Book Production* is firmly rooted in the twenty-first century and its technologies, while still bearing in mind that books are a medieval construct; and though printing has changed almost beyond recognition, and will continue to do so for some time yet, paper is still a natural raw material produced from trees, and binding is still about joining sheets of paper together to make a book.

The book is based on my own experience of working in production, and is divided into two parts. Part I is about project and production management seen from a strategic as well as an operational perspective. Part II is about the raw materials and the processes by which the raw materials are turned into a book. The accent of the book is more on what needs to be done to define and run a project, and on what needs to be done to get a book printed and bound, than on the actual processes themselves which, from a production point of view, are what the printer and the binder know all about. In this it is more like David Bann's book on production *Book Production Control* which came out in 1995, and less like John Peacock's *Book Production* which was first published in 1989 and provides a mass of highly informative and beautifully written detail on how the printing and binding processes work, as well as on how to get the most out of them. Both of these books have long been out of print, so it is hoped that the book you have before you will be seen as a worthy successor, if not a useful replacement.

Chapter 1 deals with project management and how it is used to plan and organise resources and mechanisms to produce an outcome. As with the rest of the book, case studies are used to illustrate practical points, or to make things clearer. In Chapter 2, the focus is on how the theory and practice of project management can be applied to publishing production management. It then moves on to deal with how production relates to other functions like editorial and marketing, and with outside suppliers, and concludes with how a specification is prepared, estimating, scheduling and the choice of printing processes. Chapter 3 is spent looking at the implementation of the project, which is the point at which everything that has been planned and organised is turned into action, and at how the project manager monitors progress in order to prevent the project from being delayed. The chapter discusses the issuing of production orders, and what to look for in a printer to try and find the best one for the job, before ending with the end of the project and the need for reflection as part of a process of understanding what went wrong and how to avoid the same things happening on the next project. The final chapter in this part, Chapter 4, works through the range of available options for taking simple text to the point that it can be transformed into a printed book or an electronic product. This covers conventional as well as various XML-based workflows, and there is some useful information about digital image files and their formats.

Part II starts with a chapter on raw materials, Chapter 5, which covers everything from paper, through inks, adhesives, coatings and coverings, and their effect on the environment. Chapter 6, devoted to printing, looks at what is available, from digital to litho, sheet-fed to web, single-colour to 4-colour; at printing defects and what to do when you discover that something has gone wrong. The last two chapters concentrate on binding and finishing (Chapter 7), and on getting stock into the warehouse, and the all-important subject of the legal context in which the entire project takes place (Chapter 8).

This is the only book of its kind, based on experience of and research into a rapidly moving area. What, I hope, will make it useful for you are its relevance, its practicality, and above all, its approach.

# Part I

# Production and project management

# 1 Project management

Project management is about planning, organising, monitoring and controlling the use of mechanisms and resources to produce a specific outcome. The aim of this chapter is to introduce the essentials of project management and to show how they are used in publishing.

Before starting, I would like to make it clear that although I talk about departments, publishers and organisations, what appears in this chapter and throughout the book is as relevant to a large transnational organisation as it is to a person producing their first book on their own. This is because production, like editing or design, is a publishing function just as much as it is a department. If you are that person producing your first book on your own, you will be as involved in editing, production or design issues as your counterparts in a big publishing company. The only real difference is one of scale.

We need to start with some definitions in order to understand what a project is, and the similarities between project and production management.

## What is a project?

It is actually quite hard to produce a single definition of what a project is, as definitions vary with the nature and size of the project, from large ones like building a school to small, personal ones like organising a holiday.

Nevertheless, projects do share a set of common characteristics that make them different from everyday work. A project:

- is a process made up of a series of specified activities (or tasks) used to convert inputs into outputs in order to produce the final outcome, or product
- has a defined lifespan, with a beginning, middle and end
- is usually a one-off effort, and concerned with creating something new
- operates under a set of constraints
- needs mechanisms and resources to achieve its outcome.

The constraints are:

- money
- time

- quality
- skills
- equipment
- legal
- logic
- environmental.

The mechanisms and resources are:

- people with skills, knowledge and expertise
- tools, equipment and technology
- money and time.

## A project as related to publishing and production

### Activities and tasks

In a publishing project the specified activities include the entire publishing process: upstream, from authorship through editing, design, sales, marketing, promotion, to downstream with distribution, and the final outcome being the publication of a book. Activities are broken down into tasks, which need to be allocated to members of the project team.

How the book will be edited and what it will look like in terms of size, number of pages, use of colour, whether it is to be a hardback or paperback, sewn or unsewn will already have been decided by editorial working closely with marketing.

Production is usually much more involved in the mid- and downstream activities of:

- product specification and quality management
- scheduling and time management
- estimating and money management
- supplier selection and management
- raw materials selection.

Though, as will be seen, production is effectively involved to some degree or other throughout the publishing process carrying out tasks associated with authors, editors, designers, finance, sales, marketing, rights, warehousing and distribution.

### Inputs and outputs

The inputs range from: text files, image files, raw materials such as paper, ink and board; and the output is generally a printed product. The outputs are the product of a process; for example, paper is the input to the printing process, and printed sheets are the output. Inputs and their outputs are the building blocks of the project all contributing to the final outcome.

### The project outcome

The project outcome, as far as production is concerned, is punctual delivery to the warehouse of finished stock, produced at an agreed price, to an agreed standard, and in the correct quantity.

### Project lifespan

In simple terms, a project starts when the author contract is signed, and it ends when the product is launched on publication day. For production, the start of a project varies according to how involved production is with the upstream activities of authoring, editorial, and design, providing advice, information and rough estimates; and the end comes when delivery of stock has been accepted by the warehouse.

### Effort

One characteristic of publishing is that it puts a lot of effort into creating its products, most of which are new, one-off, micro-products (there are, of course, reprints and new editions as well); and most people in production find themselves managing more than one project at a time.

### Constraints

The constraints for a publishing project are the same as those which appear in the list. However, the big difference between a publishing project and, say, building a school, is that publishing projects are usually carried out in a highly competitive, commercial environment, where there is an unremitting drive to produce new products and a premium on bringing them to market as speedily and cheaply as possible, working in the knowledge that someone else might get there before you, and produce a better or cheaper product into the bargain.

In this kind of environment time becomes speed, money becomes price, and quality can become relative. Skills, equipment and project logic are all co-ordinated to make the project move faster and cost less than one's competitors can.

Good project management understands and takes these constraints into account, working with them to minimise any braking effect on the project, and thereby gaining competitive advantage over the competition. To the victor the spoils!

### Mechanisms and resources

For the project to work successfully it needs people with the necessary skills, knowledge and expertise to carry out their specified tasks competently, quickly, efficiently and effectively. They will also need the necessary equipment, tools and technology to help them with this; and, of course, production's choice of suppliers is a critical element in the success, or otherwise, of the project.

Then there is, of course, the need for adequate financial resources, without which the project's wheels will not be able to turn properly or, at worst, not be able to turn at all; and, finally, there is the need for the right of amount of time in which to carry out all these activities.

## Project management: the theory

Project management is essentially a business process, and involves the following.

- Defining and planning a project in terms of its intended outcome, how and when this will be achieved, and at what price, in light of identified constraints and available resources and mechanisms.
- Taking the external constraints and managing them by turning them into internal procedures, policies, and objectives, which people in the organisation know about, understand and work to. So, for example, money can be managed through budgets, estimates and cashflow forecasts; time can be managed through schedules
- Making sure that mechanisms and resources are available.
- Co-ordinating the activities – authorship, editing, design, marketing, manufacturing – needed to transform inputs into outputs and, ultimately, into the finished product.

The project manager is responsible for the overall management of the project, and this involves:

- defining the project in terms of:

  o   inputs
  o   processes
  o   outputs
  o   procedures
  o   policies
  o   objectives

- reducing the project to a specified set of activities and tasks
- ensuring that the necessary resources are available as and when needed
- planning the work to be done and allocating resources to activities and tasks
- implementing, monitoring, and controlling the project
- reporting progress and problems
- closing down the project when it has been completed
- carrying out a review to establish what lessons have been learned, and how this information can be used to improve the way future projects are managed.

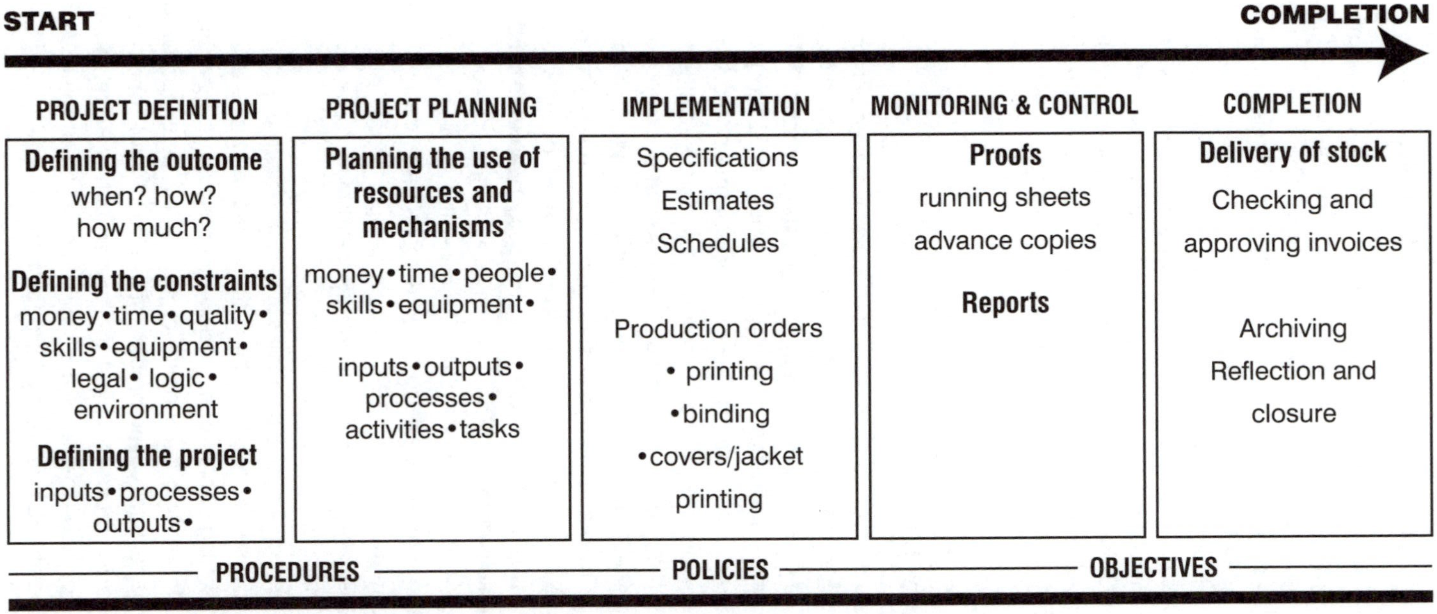

START

COMPLETION →

| PROJECT DEFINITION | PROJECT PLANNING | IMPLEMENTATION | MONITORING & CONTROL | COMPLETION |
|---|---|---|---|---|
| **Defining the outcome**<br>when? how?<br>how much?<br><br>**Defining the constraints**<br>money•time•quality•<br>skills•equipment•<br>legal• logic•<br>environment<br><br>**Defining the project**<br>inputs•processes•<br>outputs• | **Planning the use of<br>resources and<br>mechanisms**<br><br>money•time•people•<br>skills•equipment•<br><br>inputs•outputs•<br>processes•<br>activities•tasks | Specifications<br><br>Estimates<br><br>Schedules<br><br><br>Production orders<br><br>• printing<br>• binding<br>•covers/jacket<br>printing | **Proofs**<br>running sheets<br>advance copies<br><br>**Reports** | **Delivery of stock**<br>Checking and<br>approving invoices<br><br><br>Archiving<br>Reflection and<br>closure |

──── PROCEDURES ──── POLICIES ──── OBJECTIVES ────

*Figure 1.1* Project lifespan

## Project management in practice: defining the project

So far we have been looking at what happens in theory. It is now time to see how things work in practice. Defining the project in terms of its activities, inputs, processes and outputs is relatively simple. The author has produced a text (input) that needs to be edited and designed (activities), printed and bound (processes) as a book (output).

However, each project is unique, and as can be seen from the two case studies that follow, the way a project is defined, and the way it works, is influenced by the nature of the inputs, the people involved, the processes, the resources and mechanisms, and the final output. The more information can be drawn together, the more nuanced and granular that information, and the more you understand what it is telling you, the easier it is to run the project.

### Case study 1.1

This case study involves producing 350 copies in paperback of a 96-page collection of poems by a well-known poet. It was decided to publish the book to coincide with the celebration of the author's 75th birthday. Since this was a collection of the poet's work, all of the poems in the book had already been published elsewhere. Most of the text was submitted as a Word file. However, ten poems were submitted as printed copies from the publication in which they had first appeared, and needed to be converted into a digital form, either through optical character recognition (OCR) reading and scanning, or through rekeying before they could be used. There were no illustrations, and the cover was a 2-colour typographic design. As the poems had already been published, editorial inputs were limited to some light-touch copy-editing for house style and consistency, but not much more. Because the book was part of the company's poetry series and followed a series style, design inputs were light. The one major input was the cover design, as this was specific to the book. However, there was a strong brand style to follow, so inputs were fairly minimal.

The text and the cover were sent out to a freelance designer, who had been dealing with the other books in the series, and was used to handling poetry setting, which can be quite complex and, therefore, slower and more demanding than novel or biography setting. The designer submitted page and cover proofs for approval and, once these had been passed for press, supplied the printer with a Portable Document Format (PDF – see Chapter 4 for a fuller coverage of this). The author, who lived in the UK, had asked for page and cover proofs to be sent to her as printed copies, as she was not connected to the internet and was unable to receive or read digital proofs. So, time had to be allowed for proofs to travel in both directions by post. Given the light editing and the fact that the poems had already appeared elsewhere, there were only a few corrections, and only one round of proofs was required.

With only 350 copies to print on the first run, the book was an ideal candidate for short-run digital printing. However, marketing was keen for the book to be printed on a 100gsm bulky ivory-coloured paper, and to be section sewn, in keeping with other books in the series, which ruled out digital printing. (If these terms are new to you, please go to the relevant chapter in the book, where they are explained in full in their context – Chapter 5: Raw materials; and Chapter 7: Binding and finishing.)

In view of these requirements, it was decided to print the text lithographically, the cover digitally, and to bind it section sewn.

This case study appears at first sight to be reasonably simple in terms of what is known – for example, there was only one author, and her work had already been published. But it is less simple when it comes to the other factors that need to be taken into account. For example, the fact that the author was not connected to the internet and was, therefore, unable to read proofs on screen means that printed proofs (hard copy) had to be sent out and returned by post (or courier), which added time to the schedule, as well as the extra cost of organising the posting of the proofs. The fact that the author's work had already been published elsewhere may lighten the editorial load, but permissions had to be obtained from the original publishers, and this took time.

## Case study 1.2

This case study concerns a 688-page world wine atlas. The atlas was a 4-colour integrated hardback, with numerous photographs, graphs, diagrams, tables and maps. This was a multiple contributor project, with eight authors, working under a general editor. Although the general editor worked in the UK, the authors lived variously in: France, Italy, Germany, Spain, the USA, South Africa, Australia and Chile.

With the number of people involved it was decided, at the outset, that a freelance production editor would be taken on to deal with the task of co-ordinating the flow of copy and proofs between the contributors and the general editor during the writing stage. Working with the general editor and contributors, she was also responsible for:

- identifying what illustrations were required
- working with freelance picture researchers to source illustrations
- arranging for illustrations to be drawn and labelled where appropriate
- arranging for illustration captions to be written and checked.

Although the book was designed to a grid, the production editor needed to work closely with the designer to decide on the positioning and sizing of illustrations, and approve each page.

The upstream activities and inputs were identified and defined as:

- writing and approving the text, and illustration captions
- identifying and agreeing illustrations
- sourcing and originating illustrations
- design, page layout
- proof reading
- sign off.

From the outset it was clear that the only way to run the project was digitally in terms of communication, writing, illustration sourcing, creation and proofing. What was also clear was that content was intended to be re-used to produce a whole range of different atlases based on regional wines, vintage years, wine by colour, grape variety and so forth, and that to do this would require markup and tagging (see Chapter 4 for fuller explanations of these things). It was also intended to publish the main atlas and its derivatives online, as ebooks and as apps.

A further factor to consider were the co-edition deals with a French, an Italian, a Spanish and a German publisher, as well as bulk sales to a publisher in Australia and one in South Africa. The arrangements were to print and bind all the language editions in the UK, and ship them out to the various European publishers. In the case of the Australian and South African bulk deals, it was agreed that printing and binding would be done locally, thereby saving time and eliminating transport costs altogether.

In this case study, the nature of the product is more obviously complex, especially in the upstream areas involving writing, editing and design. So much so that extra resources had to be identified and brought in – a freelance editor, and freelance picture researchers and illustrators for the maps and diagrams – at the start of the project to make sure that it worked.

By comparison with the complexity of the upstream work, printing and binding were pretty straightforward.

## Procedures, policies and objectives

Whereas inputs, activities, processes and outputs change and are generally redefined with each new project, procedures, policies and objectives remain more or less stable, and are applied across the company and down into departments. They are the glue that holds everything together, and provide the necessary framework in which projects take shape and move forward. Without such a framework, project management would become virtually impossible.

### Procedures

Procedures are grounded in the day-to-day tactical operations of the company, unlike policies and objectives which are strategic. Procedures are routine ways of doing things, and they need to be understood and followed by everybody working in the company. It is also important that they are understood and followed by people working outside the company, like printers and binders, when they are engaged in doing work for the company.

Procedures are essential if staff are to carry out their tasks efficiently and effectively. They make it possible for tasks to be completed in a standard way without the need for staff to set up a framework or having to take decisions. They reduce the risk of duplication and, more importantly, the risk of mistakes. They also provide a written record of what was asked for, and how.

Procedures are best written down, and kept ready to hand, so that new staff can follow the routines correctly.

In production terms, there are procedures for:

- preparing a specification
- preparing a request for estimate from a supplier
- estimating, and presentation of estimate
- issuing production orders for:

    o   printing
    o   binding
    o   jacket/cover printing

- closing the project on completion.

Although there may be the risk of things becoming too bureaucratic, the specification and request for estimate, estimating, and all the production orders, should be prepared and presented using standard forms. This is useful in ensuring that information is presented consistently and in a standard way.

## Policies

Policies have been described as a 'set of ground rules and criteria to be applied when taking decisions relating to a particular function or activity. Thus, the existence of a policy establishes boundaries that restrict the scope and nature of decisions concerning a specific issue.'[1] Policies are guides to decision making and actions. Policies are important because, if clearly stated and correctly followed, they ensure that what people do on a day-to-day basis is compatible with and contributes to what the organisation is trying to achieve in terms of its objectives.

In production, there are policies which cover the choice and selection of:

- workflow
- suppliers
- paper
- printing and binding processes.

There are also policies which cover things like:

- the number of quotations needed for each job
- producing work in-country and overseas
- transport management
- environmental management.

Policies:

- make it possible to co-ordinate a range of activities and tasks across the company and within a department
- make it easier to delegate work, because people know the ground rules they are required to work to
- reduce the likelihood of confusion and misunderstanding.

## Objectives

For a strategy to work, it needs to be broken down into something smaller, and this is where objectives come in. Objectives are subsets of strategy, and define what the business needs to achieve if it is to succeed. A company typically has a whole range of objectives to cover all of its activities, internal and external, in relation to its:

- rate of growth
- return on investment

- market share
- introduction of new products
- competition
- efficiency gains
- impact on the environment.

Most, if not all, of these objectives will have an effect on what production does in terms of its policies and procedures – for example, return on investment and environmental impact, to mention just two.

## Activities and tasks

Now that we have defined the inputs, processes, outputs, procedures, policies and objectives, and understood how they can affect and influence a project and the way it is run, it is relatively straightforward to plan the project as a specified set of activities.

If we take the first case study as an example, the tasks that need to be carried out to take the project from a Word file and ten pages of hard copy to 350 copies of bound stock in a warehouse are:

- schedule preparation
- copy-editing*
- scanning of ten pages of non-digital text
- text design*
- blurb writing
- cover design*
- text and cover proofing
- proof reading
- correction
- specification and request for estimate*
- quotation submission*
- estimating
- preparation and issue of production orders
- PDF preparation of text and cover
- proofing
- text printing
- approval of printed output (either in the form of folded and trimmed printed sheets, or electronically)+
- cover printing
- approval of bound copies+
- delivery of stock to warehouse.

As the book is part of a series, some of the tasks may be done in reduced form, and these have been marked with an asterisk. For example, a series specification already exists, and the printer may have agreed a set of price scales with the publisher, which would reduce, or eliminate, the need to get a quotation. Items marked with a cross might be omitted altogether, depending on company policy.

## Resources

It is now time to work out what resources are required and when they are needed. It is important to remember that resources need to be available at exactly the right time. For this to happen requires a good knowledge of when everything is scheduled to take place.

Two of the biggest resources are:

- people
- money.

With people, it is important to have the right number to carry out the necessary tasks. These people need to have the appropriate skills and competencies to do the work, and they need to be in the right place at the right time. They may be members of staff, but they could just as easily be outside the company like freelancers and suppliers.

When it comes to money, making certain that:

- there is enough of it to pay for the project is done through estimating
- money is available at the right time to pay for services and goods is done through cashflow management.

In the first case study resources were used quite sparingly: in terms of *people*, there was a bit of editing to do, the text and cover design followed a series template, there was some proof reading to do, and the book needed to be printed, bound and delivered. In terms of *money*, there were permissions fees, and staff and suppliers to be paid. But costs were relatively low mainly because a lot of work that would otherwise have been involved in editing and design had already been done, and because the print run was quite small. Money, in terms of cashflow, was needed throughout the project to pay internal staff and freelancers as they completed their work on the text and cover. Suppliers submitted their bills once printing and binding was completed and, because of the 60-day credit arrangements between publisher and supplier, were not actually paid until after the book had been published, and the publisher was earning revenue from it.

There is a strong contrast between the project in this case study and the wine atlas project, where there was a lot of editorial and design work spread over a long period, as materials were created and brought together. The costs for this were high because of the number of people involved, and also because:

- the book was long and complex
- the extent (number of pages) was long

- it was 4-colour and hardback
- the print run was high.

Making sure that funds were available was critical. But even more critical was the need to know exactly *when* they were needed – too early, and they are being wasted; too late, and problems may arise. Some of the costs like paying staff salaries (including the general editor's) and freelancers were front-loaded and started when the project started and continued throughout its lifetime. Others like printing and binding, or paying the contributors (who, in this case, were paid a royalty, rather than a fee) – were back-loaded which was better for the financial health of the project. To offset these costs, money flowed into the company from the various co-edition and bulk sale deals on signature of contract.

## Project management in practice: planning the project

### *Planning the work to be done, and allocating resources to tasks*

Once all the aspects of the project have been defined, the next step is to plan the work that needs to be done, and to allocate resources accordingly. To do this, there needs to be:

- a project completion date
- nature, number, sequence (and logic) of tasks in the project
- start and end dates for each task.

With this information, it is now possible to decide how many people are needed to carry out each task, when they will start doing this, and when they will complete it and be free to start work on another set of tasks. Planning the project this way also allows you to work out when funds are needed, and how much.

At this stage you might find it helpful to use a Gantt chart (Henry Gantt 1861–1919). Gantt charts are useful for planning the use of time because they allow you to see the project as a flow of activities instead of just a series of dates. They also allow you to see where and which activities are dependent on each other: for example, printing and binding which cannot start until proofs have been signed off; and which activities can be carried out simultaneously – for example, design and layout, and jacket design and approval, making it possible to fit 26 weeks of work into 20 weeks.

As you can see in the example of a Gantt chart, activities and their duration are listed on the left, and the time frame in weeks runs across the top. The duration of each activity is shown by a horizontal bar which reflects the time allocated. In this example the proofing and sign off, printing and binding, delivery of stock to the warehouse, and order processing are all shown as being dependent on each other. Whereas the other activities – desk- and copy-editing, design and layout, jacket design and approval – are shown as running in parallel, and are not dependent on each other.

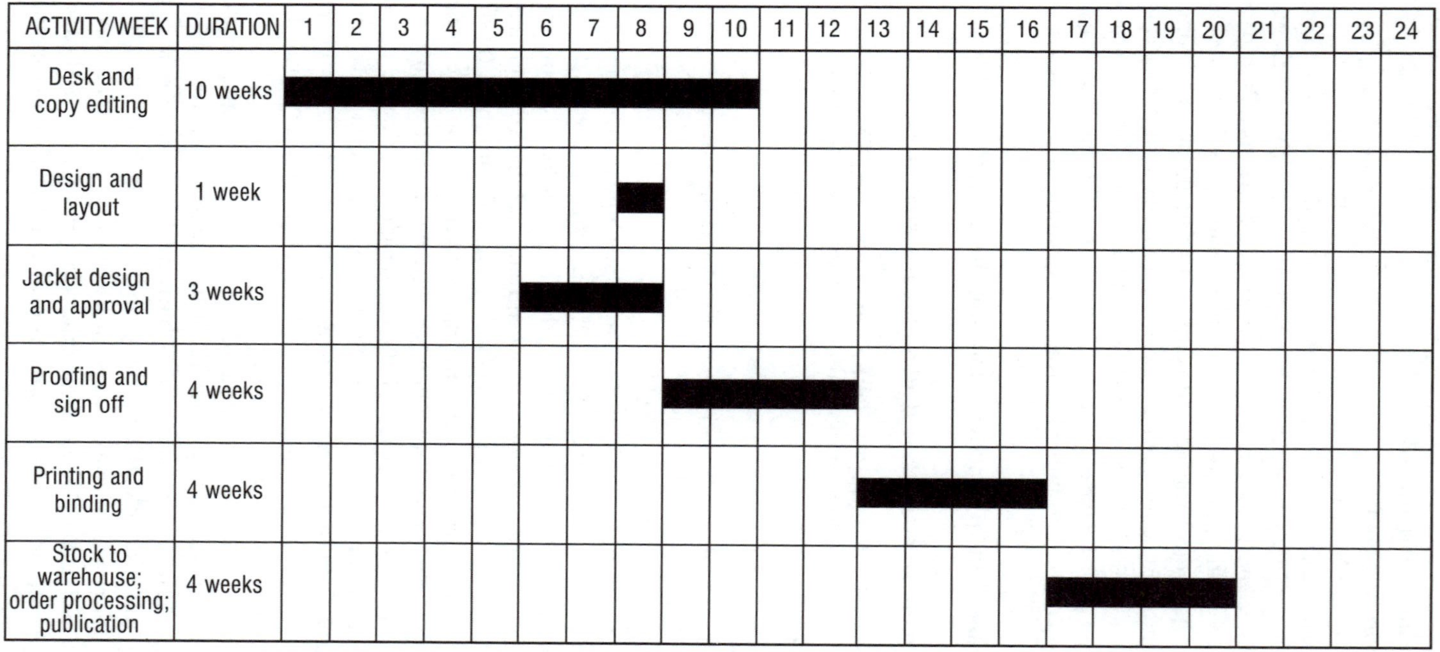

| ACTIVITY/WEEK | DURATION | 1 | 2 | 3 | 4 | 5 | 6 | 7 | 8 | 9 | 10 | 11 | 12 | 13 | 14 | 15 | 16 | 17 | 18 | 19 | 20 | 21 | 22 | 23 | 24 |
|---|---|---|---|---|---|---|---|---|---|---|---|---|---|---|---|---|---|---|---|---|---|---|---|---|---|
| Desk and copy editing | 10 weeks | ██ | ██ | ██ | ██ | ██ | ██ | ██ | ██ | ██ | ██ | | | | | | | | | | | | | | |
| Design and layout | 1 week | | | | | | | | ██ | | | | | | | | | | | | | | | | |
| Jacket design and approval | 3 weeks | | | | | ██ | ██ | ██ | ██ | | | | | | | | | | | | | | | | |
| Proofing and sign off | 4 weeks | | | | | | | | | ██ | ██ | ██ | ██ | | | | | | | | | | | | |
| Printing and binding | 4 weeks | | | | | | | | | | | | | ██ | ██ | ██ | ██ | | | | | | | | |
| Stock to warehouse; order processing; publication | 4 weeks | | | | | | | | | | | | | | | | | ██ | ██ | ██ | ██ | | | | |

*Figure 1.2* Gantt chart

In the first case study resource use was relatively light, and time could have been saved by carrying out some tasks simultaneously – for example, the cover could be designed while the text was being edited.

For the wine atlas, the human resources demand was high:

- one general editor
- eight authors
- one freelance production editor
- one in-house managing editor
- one in-house copy-editor
- one designer
- two freelance technical illustrators for diagrams and drawings
- two freelance cartographers for maps
- two freelance picture researchers
- one freelance indexer
- two freelance proof readers
- one supplier to print and bind.

The work of these people had to be co-ordinated and scheduled, so that everyone knew what they were supposed to do, and by when. The internal project logic dictated the sequence, or priority, in which tasks needed to start and be completed by, so that the output from one task was available to become the input for the next task.

So far, everything that we have covered in this section has been to do with planning a project. The next section is concerned with executing, or implementing, the plan and running the project.

## Project management in practice: implementation

Once project planning has been completed, it is time to implement the project and put the plan into action. Implementation is about making the project work so that it ends on time, within budget, and with the intended outcome.

This presupposes that the plan has taken everything into account, but is still flexible enough to work even in the face of unexpected changes. It also assumes that the plan has been communicated to everyone involved and that they are aware of their role in the project.

If this is the case, then the project is more likely to move steadily and smoothly on its course from beginning to end. However, even the smoothest projects need to be controlled, and the project manager needs to be constantly on watch monitoring and controlling what is happening to the project in terms of:

- scope
- progress
- cost
- time.

*Monitoring and controlling project progress*

Monitoring is basically about checking that things are running according to plan, and can be done in several ways – for example, by personal observation, analysis of reports, checking outputs or simply by being told.

When monitoring shows that the project is starting to deviate from the plan, it is time exercise control, by taking action to get it back on course.

The most common problems are these:

- Scope creep, which occurs when work, not included in the original project definition or plan, is introduced into the project as it is running. Unless scope creep is controlled, costs rise, delays occur, and the likelihood of meeting the target date, or deadline, is put in jeopardy. On the other hand, scope creep can be difficult to control, particularly if it is felt that the extra work is necessary, or justified.
- Cost creep, which can often be a by-product of scope creep. There is little one can do about this other than re-estimate and re-cost the project.
- Slippage: again this can often be as a result of scope creep. The best way to control this is to have allowed enough flexibility in the schedule, when it was being prepared, for it to absorb the slippage without endangering the date set for the project to end.

These problems, provided they are spotted early enough in the life of the project, are fairly easy to deal with and may only require a minor adjustment here and there. However, as the project advances and time starts to run out, they require more effort and time to resolve.

Because publishing project management involves producing something physical, and using raw materials and industrial processes to turn them into a finished product, there is a high premium on monitoring and controlling quality at as many stages in the project as possible, and certainly before an output becomes the input for the next process. As a practical example, this means that right from the start the quality of the paper (the input) must be good enough not only to produce the desired product but also to withstand the rigours of passing through the printing and binding processes. These processes run at such high speeds, and so late in the overall project, that problems with raw materials, or printing and binding processes, can rapidly escalate and have a serious, sometimes fatal, impact on achieving a successful project outcome.

## Case study 1.3

This case study concerns a 480-page, single-colour, hardback biography. Two thousand copies were printed; and immediately after printing, folded and trimmed printed sheets (also known as running sheets) were sent to the publisher to check their quality before the job moved on to binding.

On looking through these, it was discovered that the captions for two illustrations had been transposed. The mistake was corrected, and a replacement section was printed and amalgamated with the other sections. Because the mistake had been spotted early on, the problem was relatively minor, the schedule was not affected, and the book was published on time: the extra costs incurred were only for paper and printing. If the mistake had been discovered after the book had been bound and delivered to the publisher's warehouse, it could have been put right, but this would have cost a lot more, and would have delayed publication.

## Case study 1.4

This case study is about a Greek–English, English–Greek pocket dictionary. Ten thousand copies had been printed, single-colour, and it was perfect bound in a 2-colour vinyl cover. Printing was done overseas, and stock was brought overland by lorry. Running sheets had been approved, but because of the pressure of time, it was decided to forgo approval of advance copies. Copies were delivered to the publisher's warehouse in time for publication. The return of the first defective copies started about a week after publication, followed by hundreds of copies during the weeks that followed: two 64-page sections had been gathered in the wrong sequence, so that pp.193–256 appeared in front of pp.129–92. The way the book was bound, and the very tight margins on the pages, normal for dictionaries, meant that the book could not be repaired and the entire impression had to be pulped.

Controlling a project when it starts to go wrong is a critical part of project management. It requires a good understanding of the project as much in terms of its objectives, as of the inputs, the outputs, the schedules, costs and the required quality. It requires a knowledge and understanding of how the processes work, and how they can be used creatively to make up for lost time, reduce burgeoning costs or improve quality. It also calls for an ability to assess and judge a situation correctly, knowing what, and how much, action to take and when.

## Project management in practice: reporting progress and problems

Communication is a vital tool in managing the project: its value cannot be overstated. Poor quality communication is one of the commonest causes of unsuccessful projects.

Communication starts with the project definition and continues right through to completion. The more that people directly, and indirectly, involved in the project know about it, the better. Telling people – in-house staff, suppliers and other stakeholders, what is expected and what is happening, helps to manage expectations and eliminates last-minute surprises.

To be good, communication should be proactive and it should be regular: 'We're telling you how things are going, you don't need to ask.'

Communication can be done through reports, meetings, or presentations: however it is done, what is communicated needs to serve the needs of the receiver rather than the sender. It needs to be current, focused, accurate and honest. It needs to be comprehensive and provide information on all aspects of the project from resource needs to achievements, risks, and issues arising from scope change, slippage and to do with quality.

The way it is presented should be understandable to everyone concerned: people working in production, editors, the author and suppliers.

## Project management in practice: closing down the project

The final phase of the project comes with closing it down. The outcome has been achieved, the product has been successfully delivered to, and accepted by, the warehouse; and it is now time for the people who have been working on the project to start work and concentrate on the next one. Before this happens, there are certain tasks that need to be done, which mainly involve the project manager, but may also involve everyone engaged in the project.

Project closure consists of two phases:

- administrative closure
- evaluation, and lessons learnt.

In administrative closure:

- suppliers' invoices are checked against estimates, and paid; where discrepancies occur, they need to be sorted out with the supplier
- project records like specifications, suppliers' quotations, estimates and production orders are completed and filed away, archived ready for re-use in case of a reprint.

In a busy production department it may be difficult to find time to hold a formal evaluation meeting, but it is very useful, even if only for a short time, to hold a session with the people who worked on the project – in-house and external – to:

- identify and discuss project issues and problems
- discuss how they were solved
- establish what lessons have been learned, and how these can be applied for future projects.

This may seem like having to go the extra mile, but the time, not to mention the effort, the money, and, possibly, the raw materials, that may be saved by not repeating mistakes, is more than likely to make it worthwhile. It also plays an important part in helping the production department improve its productivity and performance.

Now that we have reached the end of what project management is all about in theory and practice, we're going to see in the next chapter how it relates to publishing production management.

## Note

1 Bennett, R., *Corporate Strategy and Business Planning*, 1996, Pitman Publishing, p. 5.

# 2 Production management

In this chapter we shall see how the theory and practice of project management work when applied to publishing production management. We start with exploring the role of the production department, and how this links with other departments in the publishing company and outside suppliers.

From there we look at how a book is planned in terms of:

- its physical quality – the specification
- how much it's going to cost – the estimate
- how long it is going to take – scheduling.

The chapter ends with a review of the choices of printing process.

As mentioned in the previous chapter, production should be looked upon primarily as a function, and an essential part of the publishing process. In many companies production is the responsibility of a production department, but in a small organisation responsibility for production, editing and marketing may all fall on the shoulders of one or two people, possibly in-house or even freelance. However it is organised, production has to be done by someone. It cannot be ignored.

## What does production do?

Production's job is to manage the conversion of inputs into outputs using a series of processes (usually provided by outside suppliers) so that the required number of books is available at the right time and to the required standard. As in project management, so in production management: producing a book is a project, which needs to be defined, planned, implemented, monitored, controlled and closed down when completed. Production management is about project management.

However, production does other things besides – it is the publisher's print buyer:

- asking for and receiving quotations from suppliers
- negotiating prices
- looking for cheaper, quicker and more efficient ways of producing the publisher's products.

Production is also there to provide information and advice.

Production works in two directions: internally, with departments inside the organisation from editorial, through finance to warehousing and distribution; and externally with suppliers: printers, binders, paper merchants, shippers and transport companies. Production is the point of contact between publisher and supplier, interpreting and responding to the needs of both groups.

The best way to understand how all this works is to read through the case study that follows, where it is possible to see the various ways in which production is involved throughout a publishing project.

## Case study 2.1

This case study tracks production's involvement in a publishing proposal from inception to completion for a new title for a medium-sized mind, body, spirit (MBS) publisher. This is to be an integrated 4-colour book (where text and illustrations appear on the same page as the text throughout the book, and are not bound in as separate sections), about the religious and philosophical traditions of the Indian subcontinent. The commissioning editor has been discussing the idea for this new title with other editorial colleagues and sales and marketing, and is now ready to start putting a proposal together which will be submitted to the publications committee for approval or rejection. An important part of the editorial proposal is to demonstrate the financial viability of the title in terms of:

- investment (which includes production costs)
- break-even analysis
- pay-back analysis
- price
- profitability.

### Production and editorial

Editorial is probably the department that works closest with production and over a longer period during the life of a project, than any other department in the organisation. In a sense their work is complementary. So, while editorial works to produce the content, and to make sure that it meets the criteria for successful publication, production works to produce a physical product that meets the company's standards and satisfies the market's expectations in terms of look, feel and value for money.

The first that production hears about the proposal is when they receive a request from editorial to supply costs for printing and binding a given quantity of copies based on a rough specification, which gives details of:

- format (trimmed page size)
- approximate extent (number of pages)

- use of colour (one, two, or four)
- binding style (sewn, perfect, notch/slotted/burst)
- approximate print run (several combinations may be asked for).

Production works out the costs, and sends these to editorial, for inclusion in the proposal.

If the proposal is accepted, and the project goes ahead, production's next involvement with editorial is to produce a schedule for the project. In the case of this title, the author has been given two years in which to complete the book, which is being planned as a spring rather than an autumn publication. Any schedule, at this stage, is going to be fairly loose-textured and long-term; and will probably consist of a date for the author to hand over the manuscript, a date for copy to be passed for press, a date for books to go into the warehouse and the publication date. Such a schedule would contain the following activities and the dates on which they either occur, start or finish. In the example below, the dates have been omitted, but the time allowed for the activities to take place appears in brackets.

- Author submits final copy.
- Desk- and copy-editing (allow 10 weeks).
- Design and layout (allow three weeks).
- Printing and binding (allow four weeks).
- Delivery to warehouse (allow one day).
- Pre-publication order processing and distribution (allow four weeks).
- Publication date.

This is where it would be helpful to create a Gantt chart. (This was discussed in the previous chapter, and the example there is for the most part based on the information above.)

Since this book is illustrated, the author needs to know the preferred format in which to submit any illustrations, and what to do where illustrations are only available in different formats.

With the book taking two years to write, production now has very little, if anything, to do with it. It may occasionally come up in a progress meeting. But until the writing is completed, and the manuscript has been delivered, it is an editorial project under editorial control, although the editor is already working towards the intended publication date, and will pace the work accordingly.

Once the author has delivered the manuscript and illustrations, editorial then asks production for a detailed schedule giving dates for:

- copy-edited text, and illustrations, to be handed over to design
- start and completion of proofing
- passing text and illustrations for press
- checking printed output

- checking advance copies
- stock delivery to warehouse.

Managing the project now becomes the responsibility of production, whose aim is to get the book out in time to meet the publication date.

Throughout this stage of the project, editorial and production meet regularly to review progress and report on problems and delays. Where these occur, production's role (and possibly editorial's too) is to resolve them, and make sure that the project remains on schedule.

With editing completed, and text and illustrations styled, composed and laid out, proofing starts, during which production co-ordinates the arrival, dispatch and return of proofs for correction and revise until such time that editor, author and designer are satisfied that there is no further work to be done, and that the book can now proceed to be printed.

Firm costs are also needed from suppliers, so the rough specification has to be firmed up which, now that the word count and the number of illustrations are known, should be quite easy.

The latest costs for printing and binding are sent to editorial who, after consulting with sales and marketing, decides on the final print run.

The period of often intense activity between delivery of the manuscript and the moment when everything is passed for press is followed by a relative lull during which the book is being printed, and production and editorial meet to discuss progress, as well as any delays and problems.

The completion of printing is marked by the arrival of running sheets, which need to be checked by both editorial and production before binding starts.

The end of binding is signalled by the arrival of advance copies which production and editorial need to check and approve before stock is delivered to the warehouse. As far as editorial is concerned the project has virtually ended. For production, the end of their direct responsibility for the project ends when stock is accepted by the warehouse, and becomes their responsibility.

After the level of involvement with editorial, production's involvement with other departments in the organisation may seem rather low key. Certainly, there is much less of it, but it is nevertheless just as important.

### Production and design

Although it is editorial and marketing who make the decisions about what a book should look like, design and production are both responsible for turning those decisions into the reality of a physical product.

The designer working on the text and illustrations cannot do so sensibly without taking into account the physical features of the book they are working on, which means that the designer needs to know:

- trimmed page size and format (portrait or landscape – see later)
- extent

- number of sections in the book (or pages in a section)
- treatment of illustrations: integrated, or separate sections; resolution
- use of colour
- paper quality – bulk, whiteness, finish, weight, grain, opacity
- binding style: sewn, perfect, notch, saddle-stitched (see Chapter 7 for more on this)
- cover/jacket/printed paper case.

Because all these factors influence, and are influenced, by costs, it is important for the designer to be aware of the cost parameters they are working to, and this information usually comes from production when the designer is briefed.

Knowing:

- that there is no allowance for bled illustrations (illustrations which go right up to, and effectively over, the edge of the trimmed page) means that there will be no bled illustrations
- that the book is to be printed 4/1 throughout (said as 'four-back-one'; this means that sheets are printed in four colours on one side and one colour on the other) and not 4/4 (said 'four-back-four', and meaning four colours on each side of the sheet) which means that black and white pictures will have to be planned so that they appear on the single-colour side of the sheet, and 4-colour pictures on the 4-colour side
- the bulk of the paper allows the designer to produce cover artwork with the correct spine width.

This is all the more important for freelance designers, especially those working for the company for the first time, who may be unaware of design procedures and policies.

The same holds true for freelance picture researchers, particularly when it comes to graphic file formats.

### Production and sales and marketing

Unless production is directly involved in producing publicity materials, communication between production and sales and marketing is limited to providing them with information about progress on the book towards the publication date; and on physical aspects – for example, how much it will weigh, or how bulky it is. However, sales and marketing may have a standing order for jackets and covers to be sent to them for promotional purposes as soon as they are available. They may also want review copies to send out before printing begins, and advance copies when binding has been completed.

### Production and finance

Production, as mentioned earlier, is the publisher's print buyer and is one of the major spenders of the company's money, buying in a wide range of items and services from raw materials to printing, scanning, binding and transport.

Knowing about the scale of these transactions, when they are due for payment, and their effect on cashflow, is critical to the financial health and sustainability of the company. Finance needs this information to be able to plan ahead and make sure that cash is available exactly at the point that it is needed, and not before or after. This information is usually supplied by production when it prepares the final estimate for the book, where a date is given for the completion of each task in the project.

In many companies production is also responsible for checking and approving suppliers' invoices (as well as querying and sorting out any discrepancies) before passing them on to finance for payment.

### Production and rights

The rights department are keen to take the book to the Frankfurt Book Fair to try to interest other publishers in buying either co-edition or translation rights. Although rights staff have been briefed by production on how to work out the effect on costs of more co-edition publishers joining the print run, production is available at home on the end of a phone to deal with any queries about quality, timing, logistics, costs or any production-related issues that cannot be dealt with by rights staff.

### Production and warehousing and distribution

As the project develops production is in regular communication with warehouse staff about logistics and the product itself. Warehouse staff want to know when stock is due for delivery, and who the supplier is, so that delivery details can be sorted out with the supplier, or the transport company, in advance. This is important because warehouse procedure is that unscheduled or random deliveries will not be accepted, and lorries will be turned away at the warehouse gates. The warehouse needs to know the book's weight, format (trimmed page size), bulk and the number of copies, so that decisions can be made about where to store it. This information is also important for the distribution department to calculate carton sizes and distribution costs. In this particular company, the policy is that stock must be in the warehouse one month before publication date to allow stock to be scaled out to fulfil orders at home and abroad.

### Production and suppliers

Externally production is involved with a wide range of suppliers from printers to transport companies. Most production departments prefer to build up a bank of suppliers, locally and internationally, to give themselves flexibility and greater freedom of choice, both of which are necessary in a fairly crowded market where demand can suddenly outstrip supply at particular times of the year.

For this book, production has decided to place the job with a local printer, who have submitted a competitive price, and are also known for their good quality colour work and binding.

Communication between production and the supplier is initially through the printer's representative (or rep), who visits production about once a week. During these visits several things are discussed, and may be about:

- the possibility of another job, when this is likely to be ready for printing, and when stock is needed
- the details of a specification and request for estimate
- negotiations over a recently submitted price
- the latest technological developments and their possible impact on printing in general
- paper to be used for a forthcoming job
- a disputed invoice
- a cheaper and quicker approach to a job being quoted for
- plans to increase binding capacity in the bindery through the installation of new equipment
- the improvement on a delivery date for a job.

While the rep plays a vital part in developing and maintaining relations with publishers and getting work for the supplier, it is the supplier's account executive who has the responsibility for processing and organising that work once it reaches the factory; and it is with the account executive that production works directly on a day-to-day basis once the job has gone live.

The account executive:

- prepares and submits estimates to the publisher
- organises and schedules the publisher's work as it comes into and works its way through the factory
- identifies and deals with problems.

Their work is highly focused, and has one aim: to make the project run smoothly and efficiently.

This printer offers an all-in service and will:

- print and bind the complete job
- supply paper for the book block and the jacket
- make binding cases
- organise transport and delivery of stock to the warehouse.

Once the printer's quotation has been accepted, the account executive prepares a printing and binding schedule for production, based on when the publisher wants stock to be ready by, the complexity of the job, and the number of copies to be produced.

Production now runs the project according to this schedule, making sure that everyone involved knows about it and is able to work to it. If any adjustments need to be made, this should be done as soon as possible: late adjustments cause delays and the irretrievable loss of time.

Printing, binding and cover/jacket printing orders are issued when the job is ready to go to press. These orders contain all the information the printer needs to know to be able to produce the job as required, and form the basis of the contract between publisher and supplier.

By choosing a supplier who provides an all-in service, production has not had to deal with other suppliers like binders, paper merchants or transport companies. These companies operate in much the same way to get their business as the all-in supplier. They have reps who visit publishers' production departments looking for opportunities for work, and are prepared to work with production to achieve its objectives.

## Planning the product: the specification

Although a book is easily identifiable as a book, and most books, apart from their cover or jacket, look much the same, each book is the result of a series of decisions that have to be taken by the publisher if the book is to exist. Some of these decisions are editorial and are concerned with content and how it will appear on the page; others are concerned with how the book will look and feel – its physical appearance and quality. Although content, design and appearance are all closely connected, production's interest lies primarily in the book's appearance and quality.

Usually, since product is one of the 4Ps of the marketing mix (the other three being place, price and promotion) most of the decisions about what a book looks and feels like are made by the editor, working closely with marketing, and not by production or design. It is the editor and marketing who decide that the book would do better in Royal 8vo portrait (234 × 156mm) than in any other format (for further information on formats see Chapter 5). Similarly, it is they who decide on:

- extent
- use of colour
- treatment of illustrations
- binding style
- print run.

The role of design and production is to translate these decisions into a physical product that satisfies the expectations of editorial and marketing and of the consumer; and to provide advice and solutions to problems when needed.

Production's inputs at this stage are concerned with finding a printer and binder, choosing a paper that will best suit the needs of the design, will fold easily, isn't too heavy and will allow the book to open and shut properly.

## Standardisation

Before we start looking in detail at the specification and request for estimate, and estimating, it is important to understand that a lot of publishers have standardised the ways they work in terms of:

- design
- the raw materials they use in their books
- how these are printed and bound
- how they work out the cost of a job.

This has been done to make their publishing more efficient by reducing the time and effort that would otherwise be spent in starting everything afresh with each project.

If this is not the way things are done where you work, then what follows should be useful in describing how a specification and request for estimate is created, and how an estimate is produced from a supplier's quotation. It may even be useful in helping you move towards producing a standardised system of your own. For those of you already working with standardised systems, it may be interesting to see the ideas and procedures they are based on and the amount of time and effort that can be saved by using a standardised approach.

## The specification and request for estimate

As far as production is concerned the specification is where all the decisions about the book are brought together and can be sent out to a supplier to provide a quotation for producing the book. This specification is no longer the rough editorial specification sent to production so that they could provide rough costs for an editorial proposal. This specification is heavy duty, and as detailed as it can possibly be. It is usually sent out to two or more suppliers, and the optimum time is about one month or so before the book is ready to go to press. Any longer, and prices may no longer be valid when the job is ready; any shorter, and it may be difficult for the supplier to fit the work in.

A specification should be more than just about what the book is made from and how it is to be put together. To be good, a specification needs to tell the supplier:

- what they are being asked to work from (the inputs)
- what they being expected to produce (the outputs)
- when the work is likely to start, and when it is wanted by.

The more detailed and comprehensive the specification, the more accurate the quotation.

This specification is for a 320-page hardback novel, and is being sent to a printer who is able to provide an all-in service.

---

Author: Janey Gledhilll
Title: An Afternoon by the River
13-digit ISBN: 000-0-00000-000-0
Format: 216 × 138mm (Demy 8vo; portrait [see Chapter 5])
Extent: 320 pages
Impression: First
Quantity: 3,000 copies, and per 500 copies run-on

---

This information remains constant, except for the impression, which changes to second, third and so on as reprints occur.


### Portrait or landscape?

Putting portrait after the format is a simple but very useful procedure worth following to prevent confusion over whether the book is landscape or portrait. This is because in the UK we put the height dimension first and the width second, as in the example above, which identifies it as portrait. To someone not working in the UK, 216 × 138mm means that the format is landscape. It would have to be 138 × 216mm to be portrait. If you are in the UK working with a foreign publisher on a co-edition the simple habit of putting portrait or land-scape after the dimension can save you an awful lot of bother as well as waste of time and money later on.


### Extent

The extent has to be an even number of pages: it cannot be 319 or 321. This is because a sheet of paper has two sides. Extents are usually calculated in multiples of 4, 8, 16 or 32 pages, depending on the size of the page and how many can be fitted onto the sheet on which they are being printed. If you take a sheet of A4 paper, and fold it once, you will produce a 4-page section, with 2 pages on the outer side, two pages on the inner, and a spine fold, which is important in section sewn and slotted (or notch, or burst) binding. At a pinch, it is possible to print a 320-page book in 4-page sections (80 sections in all), but to do so would be expensive, requiring 160 printing plates with 160 plate changes, and ending up as 240,000 sections which need to be to folded, gathered and sewn. It would be more economical to print in 8-page sections, with 4 pages on one side and 4 on the other (frequently known as '4 pages to view'). There would be correspondingly fewer printing plates and plate changes, and fewer sections to handle. This would result in economies of scale, which will be increased if the book is printed in 16-page sections, and still further if the book is printed in 32-page sections. The more pages printed in one pass through the press, the cheaper it becomes. However, the thickness of the paper imposes a limit on how many times you can fold it; and large sheet sizes can cause problems during folding and binding.

To avoid these, it is common to slit the sheet, so that a sheet with 64 pages printed on it, could be slit and folded as two 32-page sections.

Although multiples of 8 are most commonly used, some books, especially square format ones, can be bound in 12-, 20- or 24-page sections.

*Text*

> We will supply you with a preflighted PDF of the text [see Chapter 4 for explanation]. You to produce a set of plotter proofs for approval before printing. On approval of proofs, you to print the text by sheet-fed offset lithography [see Chapter 6] 1/1 (in black ink only throughout) on a 90gsm ivory book wove paper (you to supply). No bleeds. On completion of printing, you to submit a complete set of printed sheets, folded and trimmed, for approval before binding starts.

*Text and proofs*

The printer now knows how the text is going to be supplied, that proofs and running sheets are needed for checking and approval, and that extra time needs to be included in the schedule for this.

*Printing process*

Although the printing process for this job has probably already been discussed with the printer's rep, it is important to specify the printing processes to be used. The sheets are printed in one colour only on each side (pronounced one-back-one). It may seem odd to have to put 'black ink only throughout' when it would be reasonable to suppose that all novels would be printed in black ink as a matter of course. This may be so most of the time, but single-colour is single-colour and not necessarily black, it could equally well be dark green or red. The colour could change with each section, and still be single-colour, which would certainly cost a lot more than printing in black ink throughout.

*Paper*

Although the printer is being asked to supply the paper (which is more and more the case), you will most certainly have some idea of what sort of paper you would like the book to be printed on, and will have already discussed this with the printer's rep. During that discussion you would expect to cover such things as its:

- weight
- bulk

- finish
- shade
- grain
- foldability
- opacity
- environmental credentials and pedigree
- price.

The paper you have finally decided on is one of a range of papers that the printer has in stock. It is a standard weight for a book of this kind, and is bulky enough to make the bound book appear pleasantly chunky and (possibly) appear to be good value for money in the eye of the buyer, though not so bulky as to make it difficult to fold. The ivory shade was chosen in preference to white, as it is thought to be easier on the eyes for sustained reading. The paper has good opacity (about 90 per cent), though opacity in a novel, where the lines on each side of the sheet back each other up and effectively cancel out each other's show through, is not an important consideration.

## No bleeds

Some novels contain illustrations, and these may bleed. Where this happens, the printer needs to know, as for sheet-fed work it means using a larger sheet size than for work that does not bleed. More paper costs more, and the higher price needs to appear in the quotation before the job starts, rather than as a late extra added to the invoice at the end.

## Binding

> You to fold, gather and bind section sewn in 32s; flexiline (single-lining); printed ends 1/0 (PMS), same front and back, on 135gsm cartridge paper (you to supply); head and tail bands; plain edges; case bind in Wibalin imitation cloth over 1300gsm (2300 micron) binder's boards; rounded and backed; block on spine only in imitation gold (you to make brass from artwork we will supply); jacket wrap (you to supply); pack in bulk; deliver to our warehouse.

## Sewing in 32s

Editorial and marketing have decided that the book is to be a sewn hardback. It has been decided with the printer that sewing will be done in 10 × 32-page sections, as sewing in 32s is more cost effective than sewing in 16s. However, the ability to do this is limited by how bulky the paper is: if it is too bulky, you may not be able to fold it enough times to produce a 32-page section without creasing, especially along the spine, making it necessary to sew in 16s, which is more expensive and takes longer than sewing in 32s – something to be avoided. Sewn binding is very strong and durable, and is relatively expensive. Virtually the same strength and durability could have been achieved for less cost with notch, slotted (or burst) binding. But the production values required for the book rule this out (for the moment at least: there may be some value engineering to do when the printer's quotation is received).

## Flexilining

To stiffen the book block after it has been sewn, and to make it less floppy, a strip of expandable material, called flexiline, is attached to the spine from top to bottom. The lining is also the means by which the book block is attached to the case. Some books may be double-lined, but most books are single-lined.

## Printed ends

Endpapers (often shortened to ends) can be plain, dyed (also known as self-coloured) or printed in one, two or four colours. For this book, it has been decided that the endpapers are to be printed in a single colour (which will be specified in the binding order) using the same image (a photograph of the town where the author was born) front and back. This is simpler than the front endpaper having a different image from the back one, which would require extra care to make sure that the right endpaper appeared in the right place. The usual weight for the endpapers is 135gsm and the paper is generally cartridge which is strong enough to take the strain of being the main way of attaching the book block to the case. Endpapers can be heavier, for example 150gsm, especially if the book is a large format one, and the case is heavy. The supplier is being asked to provide the paper for the ends.

## Head and tail bands; plain edges

Head and tail bands serve a function in hand-bound books, but in the kind of binding being used for mass-produced books, like this one, they are purely cosmetic and serve no functional purpose other than to signal the high production values of the product. It is possible to have a head band only, though it is more common to have them in pairs. The supplier will provide the head and tail bands, and they can be chosen from a swatch of samples.

Most books have plain edges, but they can be coloured, marbled or gilded with a metallic foil, according to taste, the intended production values and the money available to pay for them.

### *The binding case*

The hardback binding case is to be made and supplied by the printer. The front and the back of the case are made from board, usually called binder's board, and the weight and thickness chosen here are usual for a book of this format and extent. Boards are simply called 'binder's boards', a term which has replaced the often enormous and bewildering choice that existed some years ago; and are described either by their thickness (in microns or millimetres) or by their weight (in gsm, or ounces – abbreviated to ozs). Thicker, or heavier, boards are usually used for larger format books.

Wibalin is the brand name of a thick paper material which has been embossed to look like a woven cloth, and has virtually replaced real cloth as the preferred covering for hardback cases. Real cloth is still available, but its use is limited mainly because of its expense. The colour and type of cloth are identified by a number or name taken from a swatch which the supplier should provide, and will appear in the binding order.

The title of the book and the author's name are to be blocked onto the spine in imitation gold foil. This information can also appear in silver and other metallic foils, as well as silk screen. Blocking requires a binder's brass, and this will be supplied by the printer. However, they will need to have the artwork for the lettering and design to go on the spine, and this will have to come from the designer either as a PDF or as printed hard copy.

### *Rounding and backing*

The spine of the book block is to be rounded so that it is convex (done by rounding), and backed to create a shoulder on either side of the spine. This style of case binding, as well as flat backed (also known as square backed) is quite common in the UK. When a rounded and backed, or a square/flat backed, book is opened the spine of the book block becomes concave, while the spine of the case retains its original shape. In tight backed binding (also known as fast back binding) the spine of the book block is stuck to the spine of the case to add extra strength to the book block. When the book is opened the spine of the book block and the spine of the case both become concave. This style of case binding is most often used in the USA.

### *Jacket wrap; pack in bulk; delivery to the warehouse*

The bound copies are to be wrapped in a jacket, details of which appear in the specification below.

At this stage the printer only needs to know that they are being asked to pack in bulk, and make a consolidated delivery to a single address, rather than a split delivery to two or more addresses. Precise details about how the packing should be done, and the warehouse address will be provided in the production orders. The cost of delivery should be included in the binding price, and not be charged later as an extra.

*Endpapers*

> We will supply you with a PDF of the illustration for the endpapers, which is the same for the front and back. You to print 1/0 (PMS number to be notified) on a 135gsm cartridge. Illustration bleeds.

The artwork for the endpapers is being supplied as a PDF. They are to be printed single-colour, on one side of the sheet only, using a Pantone Matching System (PMS) ink. PMS inks are used for printing spot colours and solids, and are identified by a number specific to a colour. The number is chosen from a swatch, which the supplier will let you have, and will appear in the binding order.

PMS inks cannot be mixed to create another PMS colour. So, a green PMS is green, and cannot be successfully produced by mixing a PMS yellow with a PMS blue.

The printer needs to know that the endpapers bleed, so that an oversize sheet can be ordered in.

*Jacket*

> We will supply you with a PDF of the jacket. You to print 5/0 (CMYK + PMS) on a 125gsm single-sided art; matt laminate using 12 micron OPP laminate; spot UV varnish. Jacket bleeds.

The artwork for the jacket illustration is being supplied as a PDF, and the printer is being asked to print it in five colours on one side of the sheet only. This will be done by using the 4-colour process inks – cyan (C), magenta (M), yellow (Y) and black (K); the fifth colour is to be a PMS colour, printed as a solid colour, which could not be reproduced successfully, or exactly, using the process inks. The 125gsm paper is a standard weight for a jacket paper, though a heavier one could have been asked for, especially with a larger format book. An art paper has been asked for because its china clay coating gives the paper a brilliant whiteness which can make the finished jacket look brighter and more appealing. Single-sided art paper means that the china clay coating has been applied to one side only – the side to be printed on. The other side is uncoated, plain paper. Unless it is intended to print on both sides of the sheet, there is little point in asking for a double-sided art paper: it is more expensive than single-sided, and the jacket is more likely to slip off the book, which happens less with a single-sided jacket because of the friction between it and the cover of the case. The printer knows that an oversize sheet is needed to allow for the bleed.

The jacket is to be laminated using a matt oriented polypropylene (OPP) laminate to give the jacket extra strength against tearing, and protection against scuffing and marking during the book's lifetime, particularly if it has to spend its early days in a bookshop. The 12 micron thickness, and the fact that it is oriented polypropylene, are more or less standard. To provide added interest to the jacket, the title and author's name are to be spot UV varnished, so that they shine out in contrast to the matt of the background laminate.

## Prices

Please provide prices for printing 3,000 copies, and per 500 copies run-on. Please provide prices broken down into printing text, text paper, binding and cover printing, finishing and paper.

Please note that PDFs will be ready to be sent to you within two weeks of receiving your estimate, and that stock is to be ready for dispatch three weeks later.

Everything that has been specified is now taken into account by the printer, and it is on the basis of this that the job is priced. If anything has been forgotten it won't be included, as the printer has no way of knowing what you have in mind.

The prices asked for are based on an initial print run, and so many copies run-on, the size of which should be proportional to the initial run. The run-on prices make it possible to calculate variations in quantity without needing to go back to the printer for further figures, which costs money, and wastes time, both of which have to be paid for by someone, somewhere. Using the run-on figures, it is possible to calculate the cost of 3,500, 4,000, 4,500 and 5,000 copies. It is also possible to calculate costs of any quantity needed, not just in blocks of 500: for example, 3,260, 4,105 and so on. Run-ons are useful, but their accuracy diminishes the further you move away from the initial quantity. For more than 5,500 copies you would do better to ask for a revised quotation to reflect the economies of scale. It is possible to use a run-on price to calculate the costs of a lower print run, in which case it is known as a run-back. However, its use is restricted by the fact that it becomes inaccurate the further back you attempt to go, and in the final analysis you would be advised to ask for a revised price to reflect the smaller quantities involved.

The printer has been asked to provide prices broken down according to the main processes in the job. This is common practice, giving the publisher a better insight into how costs have been built up, and most suppliers are happy to provide figures as requested. It is not sound practice to ask for or receive lump sum quotations.

What we have been working through is a fairly detailed specification for a relatively straightforward book. Although you are likely to have to deal with more complex books, the principles of specification writing don't themselves become more complex. A book, however complicated, is still a book, it is still made of paper, and it still needs to be printed, bound and delivered. What changes is the detail: plate sections for the illustrations instead of an integrated book; square backed rather than rounded and backed; 4-colour and not just black and white. A good specification captures that detail and describes it in such a way that the supplier can understand what you are attempting to do, and can give you a price.

If there is something that you don't understand, or are unable to express, talk to the supplier, and ask them to help you sort it out. It is better to do this than produce an inaccurate specification and get a wrong price in return.

## Planning the project: estimating

Estimating is the process by which production works out the costs of producing the publisher's products. Although estimating can be done whenever it is felt necessary, it is usual for production to provide two kinds of estimate.

### The rough estimate

The first is usually asked for when the editor is putting together a publishing proposal, and things are still rather vague. The editor might ask for a combination of different prices for different print runs, extents and formats, use of colour and binding styles – hardback or paperback.

For this kind of estimate, it is more common for production to do this in-house using either their own knowledge of current prices, an in-house database or a supplier's price scales.

As mentioned below, knowing the current prices for raw materials and everything to do with manufacturing and delivery is an important aspect of the print buyer's job, changing you from being reactive to being proactive, which is a great advantage when it comes to negotiating prices with suppliers. The best way of keeping this knowledge up to date, is to analyse suppliers' quotations and invoices and use these as the basis for an in-house database.

Some publishers agree prices with their suppliers for a fixed period, usually a year, during which time prices will not change whatever happens in the market. These prices are usually based on an agreed minimum volume of work over the period in question. Prices are made available to production as price scales, and all that production need do is refer to these to get prices for a job.

Asking a supplier for a quotation at this stage may well be premature, as the project may never progress beyond the initial idea. Preparing and submitting a quotation costs the supplier money. So, providing quotations for jobs that might not materialise is an expensive and wasteful occupation, with the cost of doing this eventually working its way back to the customer, and raising the supplier's prices and eroding their competitiveness in the process.

For rough estimates the convention is to use today's prices in the UK, rather than notional prices in a place where production costs may be lower than UK prices at the time of the estimate, but may not necessarily be so when the project is ready to print and bind. During the planning stage it is a wise precaution to future-proof the proposal as much as possible, and to make it work financially in a worst case scenario, which means today's prices in the UK. When the time comes to print and bind, any reduction in costs that may result from finding lower and more competitive prices than those appearing in the estimate can be treated as a bonus, and a welcome contribution to the bottom line.

### The detailed estimate

The second kind is the detailed estimate. This is produced at a point in the project's life when details are more or less final, the time is approaching when it needs to be turned into printed books, and a firm quotation is needed for doing this. Again, there are a number of ways of getting prices:

- supplier's price scales
- in-house database
- preparing a specification and request for estimate and sending it out to a supplier.

The second one is used by the editor in calculating:

- the number of copies to print
- breakeven
- pay-back
- profitability
- pricing.

For these reasons it needs to be comprehensive and accurate.

Before turning to look at the mechanics of estimating, we need to understand some of the conventions used in estimating.

Costs in estimating are broken down into two categories.

The first category is known by a variety of names:

- fixed costs
- non-recurring costs

- first costs
- development costs.

The second category is also known by several names:

- variable costs
- recurring costs
- running costs
- manufacturing costs.

### Fixed costs

Fixed costs are so-called because they are fixed, and do not change with the number of books being produced. They are called non-recurring costs, because once they have been paid they do not come back, or recur – for example, when a book is reprinted. They are also known as first or development costs because they are the first costs incurred during the development of a project.

Fixed costs are made up of a mixture of costs incurred by editorial and production. The editorial, non-production, costs are for things like:

- fees – any payment made by the editor related to the book: a reader's fee, an indexer's fee
- proof reading – paid to a freelance proof reader
- permissions or reproduction fees – paid for the use of copyright material
- artist's fees – paid to an artist or technical illustrator
- jacket/cover design – paid to an artist/designer for their design work.

Since these are editorial fees and only editorial knows about them, production must be told about them if they are to go into the estimate.

Fixed production costs are for the following.

- Composition (also known as typesetting, page design or layout): even if this is done by an in-house designer, it is conventional to charge the cost of doing this to the book, rather than treating it as an overhead. Composition costs are calculated on a per page basis.
- Corrections allowance: the corrections allowance is the cost of author's corrections that the publisher will pay for, after which the author has to pay. The allowance is calculated as a percentage of the composition cost, and is agreed between author and publisher prior to signing the contract. The allowance varies according to what is agreed on, but a typical allowance is anywhere between 5 per cent and 15 per cent. For example, a 10 per cent

corrections allowance for a book costing £1,600 to compose will be £160. Anything that costs more than that will have to be paid by the author. Even with digital setting, corrections do cost money, so a corrections allowance is a fair way of dissuading authors from rewriting their book at proof stage.

*Variable costs*

Variable costs are known by this name because they vary according to the number of books being printed and bound. They are also known as recurring costs because they recur every time the book is reprinted. The other two names denote the fact that the job is running, and that it is being manufactured. They may seem obvious, but at least they have the advantage of saying what they do, so to speak.

Variable costs are pure-production and do not contain any costs incurred by editorial. They are basically made up of the costs of:

- printing
- paper
- binding
- cover/jacket printing, paper and finishing.

These can be refined to include whatever items have been specifically asked for in the specification. For example, in the specification earlier, although the endpapers are specified as being printed the price has not been asked for as a separate price. This is because the supplier knows that there is a cost for printing the endpapers, as this has been specified, and it will be included in the overall binding price. What would be unwelcome would be not to specify that the endpapers are to be printed, and to be landed with a price for doing this after the estimate had been approved and all the financial calculations had been completed!

*The mechanics of estimating*

Estimating allows the publisher to know how much needs to be invested to produce the title (total production costs), and how much each copy is going to cost (the unit cost). As investment goes up, the unit cost comes down; or, put the other way round, the more copies that are printed, the lower the unit cost and the higher the investment.

Sometimes, where a unit cost is too high, there is a temptation to 'print up, to price down'. The unit cost will certainly come down, but at the same as that happens, the investment goes up, as does the number of copies that have to be sold. More often than not in a case such as this, the publisher is left with large quantities of stock which they are unable to sell, though they have been paid for. The wiser option is to try to reduce the unit cost through value engineering, which will be covered later.

A printer's quotation should restate the specification, so that production can see that what the supplier is quoting for is what was asked for, and can look like the one below:

Our estimate number: D5492/1
Date: 15 July 2011
Author and title: Janey Gledhill, An Afternoon by the River
13-digit ISBN: 000-0-00000-000-0
Format: 216 × 138mm (Demy 8vo portrait)
Extent: 320 pages
Quantity: 3,000 copies, and per 500 copies run-on

*Plate making, printing and paper*

From PDF files you supply, we to preflight and supply a set of plotter proofs for approval. On approval we to make plates, and print offset litho 1/1 black throughout on a Munken Pure White Vol.13 100gsm paper (we supply). No bleeds allowed for. Supply running sheets for approval.

*Binding*

We to fold, endpaper (printed endpaper: we supply), gather and sew in 32s; flexiline; trim; head and tail bands; plain edges; round and back; casebind in Wibalin imitation cloth over 1300gsm boards, block in imitation gold on spine only from binder's brass (we supply); jacket wrap (we supply); pack in binder's parcels; deliver to a single address in UK.

*Endpapers*

From PDF file you supply, we to plate and print endpapers 1/0 (PMS) on a 135gsm cartridge (we supply). Ends same front and back. Bleeds allowed for.

*Jacket*

From PDF file you supply, we to plate and print 5/0 (CMYK + PMS) on a 125gsm single-sided art (we supply); matt laminate, and spot UV varnish. Bleeds allowed for.

| Prices | 3,000 copies | 500 r/o |
|---|---|---|
| Printing | 1356.00 | 50.00 |
| Paper | 1882.00 | 298.00 |
| Binding | 2302.00 | 351.00 |
| Jacket | 1727.00 | 100.00 |

Subject to sight of discs supplied.

Prices ruling on paper at date of order.

Rachel Handy
Account Executive

Production amalgamates the supplier's costs with costs supplied by editorial, and works out the total production, and the unit, cost as shown in the example in Figure 2.1.

In this example, editorial costs are:

- editorial fees £450
- proof reading £100
- permissions fees £750
- jacket design £150

These costs were incurred by editorial, and were supplied to production by editorial. The cost of typesetting and the corrections allowance come from production.

Production takes the supplier's basic figure for 3,000 copies, and adds the 500 copy run-ons to arrive at the range of print runs asked for by editorial. Figures are rounded to two decimal places for ease of use. For example: the per copy (or unit) cost of printing 3,000 jackets is actually £0.575666667, which has been rounded to £0.58.

Generally speaking, production costs behave in a regular pattern, and it is useful to be aware of what these patterns are, mainly to build up a feel for prices, and what constitutes a good price for a job. Being aware of how prices should behave normally, makes it easy to spot anomalies or something wrong.

For first, fixed or non-recurrent costs, the cost of investment remains constant, irrespective of how many copies are being produced; the cost per copy drops proportionally.

When the book is reprinted, fixed costs should disappear, because they are non-recurrent one-off costs. However, they will recur where a publisher has decided to amortise (or spread) their cost over more than one impression.

Variable costs behave in their own way, too.

Initial printing costs are high and run-ons are relatively small, as is the case with the quote from the printer, where the initial cost for printing 3,000 copies is £1,356, and only £50 for each subsequent batch of 500 copies. Why should this be so?

Printing prices are made up of two kinds of cost: fixed costs and variable costs. Fixed costs are the costs of:

- the printing press
- platemaking.

Variable costs are for running the press.

# New book/~~reprint~~ estimate

Date: _____

To: Editorial/Finance/Marketing

Author: Janey Gledhill          Title: An afternoon by the river

ISBN: _____         Impression: First

Format: 216 x 138mm (Demy 8vo: portrait)   Extent: 320 pages    Illustrations: None

| Quantity | 3,000 copies | 3,500 copies | 5,000 copies |
|---|---|---|---|

## FIRST COSTS

| | | | |
|---|---|---|---|
| Editorial fees | 450 | 450 | 450 |
| Proof reading | 100 | 100 | 100 |
| Permissions fees | 750 | 750 | 750 |
| Typesetting | 1280 | 1280 | 1280 |
| Corrections 15% | 192 | 192 | 192 |
| Jacket design | 150 | 150 | 150 |
| **TOTAL FIXED COSTS** | **2922** | **2922** | **2922** |
| **COST PER COPY** | **0.97** | **0.83** | **0.58** |

## VARIABLE COSTS

**Printing: single-colour, litho**

| | | | |
|---|---|---|---|
| Printing | 1356 | 1406 | 1556 |
| Paper | 1882 | 2180 | 3074 |
| **TOTAL PRINTING COSTS** | **3238** | **3586** | **4630** |
| **COST PER COPY** | **1.08** | **1.02** | **0.93** |

**Binding: sewn, cased**

| | | | |
|---|---|---|---|
| Binding: sewn, cased | 2302 | 2653 | 3706 |
| **TOTAL BINDING COSTS** | **2302** | **2653** | **3706** |
| **COST PER COPY** | **0.77** | **0.76** | **0.74** |

*Figure 2.1* New book estimate

**Jacket: 5-colour, laminated**

| Printing, paper, lamination | 1727 | 1827 | 2127 |
|---|---|---|---|
| **TOTAL JACKET COSTS** | **1727** | **1827** | **2127** |
| **COST PER COPY** | **0.58** | **0.53** | **0.43** |

**TOTAL PRODUCTION COSTS**

| **TOTAL PRODUCTION COSTS** | 10189 | 10988 | 13385 |
|---|---|---|---|
| **COST PER COPY** | **3.40** | **3.14** | **2.68** |

*Figure 2.1* (continued)

If you want to know what the fixed costs are in an initial price, all you need do is subtract the cost of the run-ons from the overall price. Working with the figures from the case study above, the initial printing cost for 3,000 copies is £1,356. The run-on price for 3,000 copies is £300 (6 run-ons of 500 copies each = 6 × £50). Subtract £300 from £1,356, and the result is: £1,056. The fixed costs for this job are £1,056, and the printing cost is £300.

Wanting to know this may seem rather strange but, as a print buyer, knowing how to do this and understanding and knowing your way round current prices is essential if you want to be able to negotiate from a position of strength when you start negotiating prices with suppliers: the more you know and understand how prices work, the better negotiator you become.

Paper costs are generally discounted between one per cent and two per cent; the longer the print run the better the discount. In this case study, there is only a difference of two per cent between the cost of paper for 3,000 and 5,000 copies. The reason for this is that paper, when bought from the printer, doesn't really have fixed costs in the same way that printing and binding do, so the difference is often very small, as is the case here.

Binding costs do not have the same run-on advantage as printing does. This is because binding is a labour- and equipment- intensive operation, involving folding, gathering and finishing, the equipment that does all these things, and the crews to run it.

Prices for jacket and cover printing behave in the same way, though they do include paper and finishing, so the run-ons are less visible.

The estimate is sent to editorial and marketing who, on the basis of the figures it contains, decide the number to print and the recommended retail price. They also become the basis on which production and finance can track the build-up of costs against the title, and approve and pay invoices.

## Pricing the product

Fixing the price at which to sell their products is the responsibility of editorial and marketing. While they make their decisions based on the cost of getting the products made, this is not the only factor they consider.

As already discussed, production costs consist of those costs which can be directly attributed to the *physical* development and production of the book. They do not take account of the company overheads: for example, the cost of running the production department or distributing the products once they have been published. So, these need to be factored in, as well as other costs like trade discounts and royalties.

However, while editorial and marketing need to be aware of all the costs involved in bringing their product to market, and not just production costs, their two overriding concerns are:

- how competitors are pricing similar products
- what the consumer is prepared to pay.

Seen in this light, it is clear that pricing cannot be just a simple arithmetical cost-plus calculation.

So, what can be done if production costs are too high, and it looks as though the project won't be approved?

## Reducing production costs

There are three options available to production to bring down costs.

### Negotiation

The first option is to negotiate with the supplier. Successful negotiation is based on a good knowledge of current prices for raw materials and processes, as well as on a wide range of non-price-related factors, which include:

- the kind of relationship you have with the supplier
- how busy the supplier is (supply and demand)
- how much the supplier wants the job
- whether it is a buyer's or a seller's market
- both parties knowing when to compromise
- both parties wanting to end up with a result they both feel satisfied with: win–win and not win–lose
- being fair, open and honest
- knowing from the start what you want, and what you are prepared to accept
- preparation of your strategy.

## *Value engineering*

The second option is to re-examine the value of the product in a process known as value engineering, or VE. The value of a product is most easily and usually judged by comparing the product's function – what it does – with what you paid for it. The idea behind value engineering is either to improve the function, and make the product better value, or to reduce the cost without reducing the function, and it is the latter that is most usually used by production.

When it comes to books, value engineering can be applied at most stages during the development process from writing right through to design: formats can be changed, extents reduced or extended, and pictures added or taken out. As the book takes shape this becomes less easy, so that by the time it gets to production, the options for value engineering are relatively limited and confined in the main to raw materials and processes, and then really to paper and binding.

Nevertheless, value engineering even at this stage can have a significant effect. For example, a publishing company planned to produce 8,500 copies of a 992-page 4-colour book on veterinary medicine on a 100gsm coated paper which would ensure maximum quality reproduction of colour-critical images. However, it was discovered that the price of this particular paper was so high that the book would have to be priced higher than a similar book published by a competitor. In addition the book weighed just over 3kg (or 6.6lbs), which made it heavy and unpleasant to use other than when read on a table, and expensive to transport and distribute. The book was also unnecessarily bulky at 79mm.

Production suggested using a 70gsm double blade coated paper whose whiteness, brightness and opacity were comparable with those of the 100gsm paper. The result was that not only was the weight of the book reduced from 3kg to 2kg (4.4lbs), but the bulk was reduced to 55mm, and there was an associated, and welcome, reduction in the cost of paper.

In binding, it is possible to use notch binding instead of sewn without affecting the function. This is also true of perfect binding, especially with the modern adhesives now available. However, there is the risk that the purchaser may perceive the value of the product as having been reduced by binding the book this way, and may be reluctant to buy it.

If we look at the options available to production for value engineering the book which appears in the case study, they would be to use:

- a lighter weight paper – probably an 80gsm wood-free paper, which would contain a small amount of mechanical pulp
- a white rather than an ivory shade
- slotted rather than sewn binding
- lighter weight boards for the case – 1100gsm instead of 1300gsm.

In addition, it would be possible to drop the:

- head and tail bands
- printed endpapers in favour of plain ones
- spot varnish on the jacket.

The object of value engineering, as seen in these examples, is all about reducing cost without affecting function. Using lighter weight paper and notch binding still allows the book to work as well as it would have had it been printed on a heavier paper and sewn.

The skill of value engineering is to know when you have reached the point beyond which function, and hence value, is being eroded by the cost-cutting changes you are making. When that happens, value engineering becomes counterproductive.

### *Find a cheaper supplier*

The third option is to find a supplier who is prepared to do the job for a lower price. Although this might immediately suggest going overseas for manufacturing, it does not necessarily have to be so, as there are suppliers in the UK who are able to provide good quality work that is just as competitively priced as work produced by suppliers in Europe, India, the Far East or the USA, with the added advantage that you don't have to add extra time to the schedule to bring it all the way back from, say, Hong Kong. The five to six weeks this takes can be the deciding factor if you are producing books using business models like print on demand (POD), or just in time (JIT).

Two other advantages are:

- the reduction in book miles – for example, 68 miles from Chippenham to Oxford, compared with 6,007 miles from Hong Kong to Oxford
- the reduction in transport and shipping costs, which can be offset against the price differential between printing in Hong Kong and Chippenham.

Given that printing has peaks and troughs which depend on patterns of supply and demand, it is more likely that you will get a lower price for doing a job when a supplier's order book is relatively empty than when it is working flat out.

Nevertheless, despite the book miles, and the time needed to bring stock back, printing overseas does have its attractions:

- prices are usually very competitive
- quality is good
- communication and service are good
- deadlines are met.

### Planning the product: scheduling

We now come to the final part of planning the product: working out the amount of time it will take to complete it. This is done through scheduling. As with estimating, many publishers use scheduling and project management software which makes this relatively quick and easy to do. What follows describes the principles of scheduling manually, which are what the software is based on. If you don't use a computer to do your scheduling for you, then this section will be helpful. If you do use a computer, what follows may provide you with some insights into the principles underlying the software.

### Time as a resource

Time is a critical resource that publishers need to manage carefully, because, unlike money, time cannot be saved up or stored; once lost, it cannot be retrieved.

However, you can make up for lost time by:

- doing things faster
- taking short cuts
- cutting out a process or function
- putting more people on the job
- spending more money.

These are all options, but the first three carry an element of risk, and if things were to go wrong as a result they could well delay the project more than if things had been left as they were; and the last two are likely to result in extra costs.

So, the best thing is to manage the use of time by:

- planning and organising how it is to be used
- monitoring how it is being used
- controlling its use when the schedule starts to come under pressure.

### Draft and working schedules

Schedules, like estimates, are produced at various points during the project's life. Usually, the first time a schedule is asked for is when editorial starts collecting information for a proposal. This schedule is a draft schedule, and is based on production's knowledge of the average time it takes to produce a particular product, and information supplied by the editor about:

- when the author hopes to submit their final copy
- a publication date which could be as much as two or three years away.

The next time a schedule is asked for is when the proposal has been approved, and the project goes live. This schedule, known as the working schedule, is more detailed, showing actual dates for tasks and events, which reflect the speed the project needs to move at to finish on time, the availability of resources (people, money, raw materials, processes) and when they are needed.

Schedules, whether draft or working, are a vital tool in project and production management because they allow a publisher to manage the time it takes to produce a product.

But schedules do more than that. They make it necessary for production to think through and test the logic of the entire project in terms of all its components and how they fit together before it even starts. They also make it possible for:

- sales and marketing to plan promotion and publicity activities connected with the book, like author signings, reviews, media coverage on TV or radio, and the production of publicity materials to coincide with these
- finance to know when suppliers' invoices are due for payment so that finance can better manage the company's cashflow
- the warehouse, distribution and booksellers to know when stock is going to be delivered.

With so many people involved in doing so many different things, their work needs to be co-ordinated, and the best way to do this is through the schedule. The more detailed and comprehensive a schedule the better it is.

It is difficult to imagine anything more awful than a project without a schedule, or with a schedule that is out of control.

### Creating a working schedule

The first thing to be decided is whether the schedule is going to be a long-term publication schedule, or a short-term production one. The long-term publication schedule includes dates for everything from the author starting work on their manuscript to:

- editing
- design
- picture research
- proofing
- passing for press, and submission of PDF file
- printing (text, illustrations, cover/jacket)
- binding
- delivery of stock to warehouse
- publication.

Because it is long-term, perhaps covering two or three years, a publication schedule is quite likely to need revision, particularly in the early stages of the project. However, as the project moves closer to publication, the need for revision should be kept to a minimum.

In a short-term production schedule, you would expect to see dates for:

- passing for press, and submission of PDF file
- printing (text, illustrations, cover/jacket)
- binding
- delivery of stock to warehouse
- publication.

This kind of schedule, partly because it covers a much shorter period, and partly because it is relatively much closer to publication, is less susceptible to revision without creating the possibility of a delay in publication.

To be good, a working schedule needs to be:

- realistic, workable and achievable – allows a realistic and reasonable amount of time for everything to be done
- complete – includes all the project inputs, outputs, events and processes
- logical – reflects the sequence of events as they appear in the project design
- flexible – has enough inbuilt flexibility to allow for small delays without breaking down
- known about, agreed to, and understood by everyone involved.

A schedule that is not all of these things will be very difficult, if not impossible, to operate.

A useful acronym often used in relation to schedules is SMART, which stands for:

- Specific
- Measurable
- Attainable (or achievable)
- Relevant
- Time bound.

To create a schedule it is common practice to work backwards from the publication date towards the beginning of the project. Doing it this way produces a more even schedule than if you start at the beginning and work towards the end. Schedules created that way often show a tendency towards having everything squeezed into the final stages, often at risk to the project!

You also need to leave out Saturdays, Sundays and public holidays, or their international equivalents when you send work to be done overseas.

The schedule should also reflect the company policy on the amount of time stock needs to be in the warehouse prior to publication. In some companies, stock can be delivered and published straight away. While in others it has to be delivered a given time before publication to allow advance orders (or subscriptions) to be processed, and to ensure that stock is received by those who have ordered copies in time for publication.

How long it takes to print and bind your books depends on a number of factors, as outlined below:

- the technology being used: producing books digitally is faster than producing them by offset lithography (analogue) – for example, it is possible to print and bind a single copy of an 896-page book in under a minute. Web printing is faster than sheet-fed, but not necessarily appropriate for your job. (See the later section on choices of printing process.)
- the nature of the product: complex books – for example, a 1,024-page 4-colour encyclopaedia – take longer to print than a 256-page monochrome novel.
- the quantity to be produced: a long run takes longer to produce than a short one.
- where it is being produced: if you are printing in the Far East or India, you need to add at least six weeks to the schedule for the time it takes to ship stock back to the UK. If you are printing in Europe, allow at least ten days to two weeks.

What this means in practice is that, if books are being produced digitally, time can be measured in days or even hours. For analogue work, you can expect anything from two weeks (ten working days) for a medium-sized print run of 3,000–10,000 copies to a month for a long-run or complex job.

A great deal will depend on:

- the way the project has been organised
- what arrangements have been made with the printer.

*Case studies*

To illustrate these points, it is helpful to look at these case studies. Case study 2.2 is for a UK-based production schedule, and Case study 2.3 is for the same book but printed overseas. In each case the editorial and design work on content is just about to be completed.

## Case study 2.2: a UK-based production schedule

A publisher is planning to produce 100,000 copies of a 448-page 4-colour integrated, hardback book on the wildlife of the polar regions to tie in with a 10-part TV series due to start on 19 October. Publication has been set for 20 October.

A UK-based offset printer, well known for the quality of their colour work and their ability to handle jobs of this size, has submitted a quotation, which has been accepted.

With editorial and design nearly completed, production and the printer met in mid-May to discuss and agree on a production schedule which reflected the:

- publisher's requirement for stock to be delivered to the warehouse four weeks before publication

- printer's need to have capacity, paper and other raw materials available for the job when they are needed
- date on which the PDFs of the various components of the book (text and illustrations), printed paper case (PPC) and jacket will be submitted.

This is what the schedule looked like:

*Table 2.1* Case study 2.2 schedule

| | |
|---|---:|
| Final PDFs of text, illustrations, PPC and jacket to production from design | 29 July |
| Final PDFs of text and illustrations, PPC and jacket out to the printer | 1 August |
| Plotter proofs with publisher for approval | 5 August |
| Approved plotter proofs back at printer | 10 August |
| Printing starts | 15 August |
| Printing completed | 26 August |
| Running sheets arrive for approval | 29 August |
| Running sheets approved | 29 August |
| Binding starts | 30 August |
| Binding completed | 16 September |
| Advance copies for approval arrive | 17 September |
| Advance copies approval given | 19 September |
| Stock to warehouse | 21 September |
| Publication date | 20 October |

Notice that the plotter proofs are shown as 'with the publisher' and 'back at' the printer's. As proofs are being sent by post, it is important to specify where they are supposed to be to avoid misunderstandings and possible delay. If proofs are being sent by email, or are being viewed online, the issue doesn't really arise.

In this case study the time allowed for printing was four weeks which, given the amount of advance warning and the time between discussion and the start of printing, allowed the printer time to procure raw materials, and ample time to complete the job comfortably on schedule.

## Case study 2.3: an overseas production schedule

If the same job had been done in the Far East, six weeks would have to be added to the schedule to allow for the time it takes to ship stock back, and the schedule would then have looked like this:

*Table 2.2* Case study 2.3 schedule

| | |
|---|---|
| Final PDFs of text, illustrations, PPC and jacket to production from design | 21 June |
| PDFs of text and illustrations, PPC and jacket to the printer | 23 June |
| Plotter proofs with publisher for approval | 28 June |
| Approved plotter proofs back at printer | 3 July |
| Printing starts | 8 July |
| Binding completed | 5 August |
| Stock ready for shipping | 10 August |
| Stock arrives at warehouse | 21 September |
| Publication date | 20 October |

Time could be saved at the beginning if the publisher had been willing to receive and approve proofs by email, or view and approve them online using a web-based FTP site. Doing this would have cut out the time and cost involved in sending (and possible returning) proofs by courier. In the end, in order to save time, and because the printer had been used several times before, it was decided to do without running sheets and advanced copies.

Again, working to this schedule the job could be completed within the allotted time.

## Case study 2.4: an overseas schedule which overran

In one case study involving printing in India, the schedule had slipped to the point that there was not enough time, before the book was to be published, for the stock of 10,000 copies to be brought back by ship. It was decided to airfreight half the stock to fulfil immediate needs, and to send the balance by sea: an exercise which ensured that stock was available the day the book was published, while at the same time costing more than had originally been saved by sending the book to be printed in India in the first place.

*Putting the schedule together*

Once you have worked out:

- all the tasks involved
- the time each one will take

- which are dependent on each other
- which can run in parallel
- resource and time constraints

you can start putting the schedule together, which can be done by listing each task and putting the start and completion date against it, like the schedules in the case studies above, or you can use a Gantt chart if you prefer to see the schedule as a series of related activities, and not just a list of dates. (See Chapter 1: Project Management for an example and discussion on Gantt charts.) Normally, though, it is customary to present the schedule as a list of activities and dates, and not in Gantt chart form.

As you work on the schedule make sure you leave some slack between tasks to allow for one or two deadlines to be missed. Arnold Bennett, writing in *How to Live* (1925), said: 'A first-rate organizer is never in a hurry. He is never late. He always keeps up his sleeve a margin for the unexpected.' Wise advice, especially the last sentence: it is not necessarily a good idea to reveal how much time you have kept up your sleeve, as it will be reduced rather more quickly than you think, once people know about it and think it is alright to miss a deadline, safe in the knowledge that in doing so they aren't going to damage the schedule.

Once the schedule has been completed, it should be circulated to everyone concerned – internal as well as external – so that they are aware of:

- what the project timeline is
- their part in the project
- what they being asked to do
- by when.

## Planning the product: choosing the printing process

As mentioned above, the technology you choose has a direct effect on how long it takes to complete a job. Digital printing, whether print on demand (POD) or short run, is capable of producing bound books extremely fast. The emphasis has hitherto been on monochrome work, but recent and ongoing developments now make it possible to produce good quality colour work digitally. This, coupled with the fact that the economics of digital printing have significantly raised the number of books that can be printed more cheaply than offset, makes digital printing a very attractive alternative to offset printing, even for first impressions. Where it was once more economical to print books by offset in a run of more than 350 copies, that number rose to 850 copies. It has recently exceeded 1,500 copies, and is still rising. Of course, fitness for purpose, price and final quality have to be taken into account, but where the differences between the two processes are only marginal, digital is already a strong contender for any form of print-on-paper work.

For offset, or litho, or lithographic, printing – the names can be used interchangeably – there are two options: sheet-fed or web.

*Sheet-fed litho/sheet-fed offset*

Sheet-fed offset is used for short- to medium-run work, for monochrome as well as colour. It is also useful for non-standard formats. The presses tend to run at lower speeds than web presses, and the printed output is a printed sheet of paper, which needs to be folded before it can become part of a book.

*Web litho/web offset*

Web offset is used for long-run printing, and produces excellent results for both monochrome and colour. The presses are capable of running at speeds as high as 50,000 impressions (or cut-offs) per hour, compared with sheet-fed press speeds of 12,000 impressions per hour. In addition to their speed, web presses also produce folded sections, which cuts down binding time. However, with the advantages come some disadvantages, as detailed here.

- A limited range of formats is available.
- Printing direction is always long grain, so producing long-grain books can be a problem. A long-grain sheet folded once becomes short grain. If folded again, it reverts to long grain, and so on. In an A5 book (210 × 148mm, portrait) printed in 16-page sections from a 640mm wide reel with a cut-off of 450mm, the sheet is folded three times and produces a short-grain section. (see Figure 5.1 on p. 112)
- Paper wastage is higher than with sheet-fed presses.

## Implementation

We have spent the last two chapters looking at planning and organising a job going through production, and at everything that needs to be done to make sure it runs smoothly and turns out the way it was originally intended. In the next chapter we are going to look at how what has been planned and organised is put into action, and how a job is actually run when it goes live. This is the real stuff of production, the place where what you have been planning and preparing is tested often to its limit and sometimes even beyond; where, in a busy production department, you might well be dealing with not one project at a time but 50 or 80 or more, in the form of new books, with a further 120 in the form of reprints, all moving at different speeds, with different needs and problems, all requiring different decisions and actions to keep them up to quality, on budget and on schedule!

# 3   Implementation

The focus of this chapter is on implementation, or putting into action, everything that has been planned and organised. Implementation is about making things happen, about monitoring what is happening, and controlling things when they don't go as planned.

I shall start with what to look for when choosing a printer for a job. It has already been decided what processes are going to be used for the job – digital, litho; sheet-fed, web; sewn binding, perfect binding. But what do you look for when choosing a printer to make sure that you are choosing the right one for the job?

We then deal with issuing production orders, before moving on to how to monitor and control progress.

The chapter ends with procedures for closing down the job once stock has been delivered:

- checking invoices
- making sure that files are up to date for a reprint
- reflecting on the project lessons learned.

The first thing to understand is the context in which implementation takes place. Prior to this, most of one's effort is focused on planning and preparing things so that the project goes to plan, and starts and finishes without any problems, leaving you time to turn your attention to other things, like planning another job. Until the project is implemented it is inactive; at that moment it goes live.

When this happens, you are working in real time, against the clock. You are working at the speed defined by the schedule, with different groups of people – editor, designer, author, printer, binder – carrying out their allotted tasks by the agreed time to an agreed standard, all of which have been defined during the planning stage.

As the project progresses, time decreases and the level of risk increases. This is best illustrated by what I (perhaps immodestly) call Bullock's Funnel.

In the diagram (Figure 3.1), a funnel (which is used to guide liquid into a narrow necked container) lies on its side. The funnel represents the publishing process from when it starts to the point that stock is safely delivered to the warehouse. On the left of the funnel, just outside the mouth is where the process starts and, depending on the nature of the job, includes:

- commissioning
- authorship
- design
- proofing
- picture research
- copy-editing
- permissions
- contract.

On the right of the funnel, where the tube ends, is the point at which stock is in the warehouse. The *x* axis, along the bottom represents time, and the *y* axis on the left represents impact.

The job of the project manager is to co-ordinate all the upstream prepress activities mentioned above, and to ensure that they all converge into a single line, which is the project, and will pass through the mouth of the funnel, along the tube, and out the other end as bound stock.

At the beginning of the project, where the lines appear at their most chaotic, there is ample time to do everything needed to create and develop the project and its content. At this stage the likelihood of mistakes and the need to put them right is quite high, but the impact these mistakes will have on the project is relatively low. If things are to be tried out, thought about, rejected and tried again, this is the perfect place and time to do this.

By the time a single line has been produced from the many, the time left begins to decrease, and the level of risk starts to rise. Once the line enters the tube, which is where printing, binding and delivery take place, pressure builds up and the project starts to move with increasing speed to its completion. Time is in short supply and the level of potential impact rises rapidly. If something were to go wrong now, the effect on the project is going to be much more serious than if it had gone wrong earlier on.

The production/project manager who knows this, and the fact that they need to be especially vigilant in the later stages of a project's life, is more likely to bring the project to a successful conclusion than one who assumes that in a project all things are equal.

Although it is not possible to eliminate all risk, it is certainly possible to minimise it by choosing a supplier who is capable of doing the job, and with whom it is pleasant to work.

## Choosing and dealing with suppliers

When you want to get prices for printing and binding your job, unless you are already working to a printer's scales, it is quite usual to send the specification

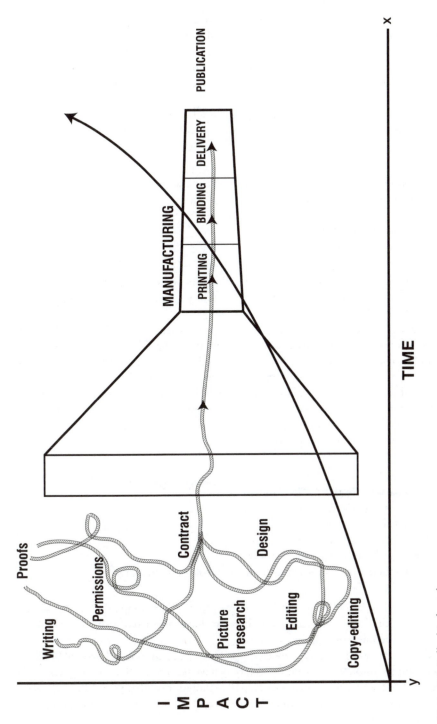

*Figure* 3.1 Bullock's funnel

and request for estimate out to two or more suppliers. If you are working with printer's scales, you have probably worked with the printer before, and know them well enough to have agreed a set of price scales in return for a guaranteed amount of work. But what happens when you haven't worked with a printer before? How do you know what they are like, and that they are going to be able to do your work properly?

There are several ways of finding out about printers.

The first is to go to their website. It is possible to judge quite a lot by just doing that.

- What does the website look like in terms of design?
- How easy is it to navigate?
- How up to date is it?
- How customer friendly is it?
- How informative is it?

You should also be able to find out what kind of equipment the printer has, and how new it is. You might also be able to find out who the printer has worked for.

The second way to find out is to meet a representative and discuss the kind of work you have in mind. The representative should be able to show you samples of previous work, a list of plant and equipment, and tell you anything that you need to know about their company: who they have worked for, and the kind of work they specialise in. If possible, it is worth arranging a visit to the printer to see the factory and things for yourself first-hand: it is possible to tell quite a lot about a printer from first impressions, and from trying to find answers to the following questions.

- How well were you received?
- How smart are the factory and its surroundings?
- How busy is the factory?
- How tidy is the factory?
- How new is the equipment?
- How well laid out is the factory?
- How efficient and motivated does the workforce appear?

The third way is to talk to production people in other companies, and ask them what they think of a particular supplier. Production is a fairly small community, and most people are willing to do this.

The fourth way is to go to a bookshop. There you can look at books like the one you want to produce and see how well they have been printed. If you like what you see, find out who the printer was (usually, though not always, on the title verso (the back of the title page); and, if not there, then at the back of the book), and get in touch with them.

Effectively, what you are trying to find out is what the printer can do (its capability) in terms of:

- prepress work
- printing
- binding and finishing
- shipping and transport.

You also want to know about its capacity, what its prices are like, and the quality of its:

- work
- service.

With the increased awareness of environmental and green issues, you would want to know how green your printer is in terms of how it manages its impact on the environment. This could be through an accredited environmental management system (EMS), which has been certified to a recognised standard such as ISO 14001. Or it could be that the printer has reduced its emissions of volatile organic compounds (VOCs) from printing, uses recycled paper, is FSC (Forest Stewardship Council) certified and has policies for waste recycling and energy reduction.

You can either choose a supplier who does everything under one roof, or a trade supplier who specialises in one of the processes only – for example, printing. Trade suppliers tend to be cheaper than suppliers who provide a complete service. However, you should be aware that you are responsible for arranging the movement of printed sheets from a trade printer to a trade binder. There are also extra costs of moving stock from one place to another, and you need to include these movements in the schedule.

So, what makes a printer good? A good printer is one who is able to produce good quality work at prices you like, who understands your business and your needs and what you are trying to achieve, who makes working with them enjoyable and stress-free, whom you like and whom you trust. The good printer will work with you to try out different approaches to producing your products, its equipment and machinery are up to date, the people you deal with there are positive and can-do, they are reliable and look after your interests. Good printers are the ones you go back to time and again, once you have found them; and I speak from my own experience, having worked with two printers for more than 30 years!

Even though finding new printers may often be necessary, it can be quite a challenge, and developing a new relationship has its hidden costs in the early stages as you get used to each other's ways of working. Nevertheless, it is a good idea to have a pool of printers to work with, each offering the same as well as different capabilities, rather than relying on only one or two.

Once you have satisfied yourself that your supplier can produce your work to the required standard at an acceptable price, and can complete the job within the necessary timescale, the next step is to place the job, and this is done through the production orders or purchase orders.

## Production orders or purchase orders

Most publishing companies use some kind of production order to place their work with suppliers, and many of them are sent by email, and are part of the Job Definition Format (JDF), which is discussed in detail in Chapter 4 on pre-press. Production orders are based on the information which originally appeared in the specification and request for estimate, and make everything specific, as shown in the examples later, which are based on the book which featured in the case study in Chapter 2 on production management. Production orders are important documents, used to transmit information from the publisher to the supplier, who uses it to issue work instructions to the crews who run the printing presses and the bindery. The production order is the contract between publisher and supplier and, as such, is a legally binding document, which is the main point of reference when problems arise between the two parties. So, they need to be accurate and complete; what you ask for in a production order is what you get. The information contained in the production orders becomes the basis of the archive for reprints and future editions.

There are usually separate orders for:

- printing
- binding
- jacket/cover printing.

If everything is being done by one supplier, it is usual to send all the orders in one batch. Otherwise, for trade suppliers, they need to be sent out individually, and well enough in advance of the job to allow them time to schedule work in.

## The printing order

A print order will typically contain the following information:

---

### CHARLES BRAND PUBLISHING

14 Headington Avenue, Oxford OX3 8AB
Phone: +44 (0)1865 971885
Mobile: +44 (0)774 501 6654
Email: cbrandpublishing@oxfordpublishing.com

*Printing Order New book/~~Reprint~~*

Date: 22 August 2011
To: Ferndale Printers Ltd, Station Road, Eynsham, Oxford OX33 1PJ

**Please print 2,750 copies** Your quotation D5492/3 dated 12 August 2011 refers

**Author:** Janey Gledhill
**Title:** An Afternoon by the River
**ISBN:** 000-0-00000-000-0
**Impression:** First
**Trimmed page size:** 216 x 138mm (Demy 8vo; portrait); no bleeds
**Extent:** 352 pages
**Process:** sheet-fed offset litho – 1/1 in black ink only throughout. From PDF supplied.
**Paper:** 80gsm Huntsman white book wove (no bleeds)
**Sheets to be printed by:** 5 September 2011

On completion of printing, please send ONE set of folded and trimmed running sheets to Lizzie Yates at the above address for approval before binding starts.

Signed
Lizzie Yates
(Production Controller)

In addition to information about addresses and the details of the book, information is included about:

- The estimate number and the date it was issued. It is important to make sure that the estimate number which appears in the production order is the latest version, and reflects any changes from the original specification. Since the supplier's invoices are based on estimates it makes sense to tie the job to the estimate relevant to the job. In the case of this book, there were three estimates which reflected changes in extent and the raw materials. In the specification the extent was originally 320 pages, and it has now increased to 352 pages; the paper has also changed from a 90gsm ivory book wove to an 80gsm white.
- The date for printing to be completed, which should reflect the date in the project schedule.

## The binding order

The binding order contains information about the book, as well as a lot of procedural information about packing and delivering stock. As can be seen, this order contains a wide range of alternatives covering everything from sewn case binding to perfect bound paperbacks (refer back to Chapter 2 for fuller details). Having a binding order arranged like this makes it easier to complete and reduces the likelihood of something being forgotten and missed out.

# CHARLES BRAND PUBLISHING

14 Headington Avenue, Oxford OX3 8AB
Phone: +44 (0)1865 971885
Mobile: +44 (0)774 501 6654
Email: cbrandpublishing@oxfordpublishing.com

*Binding Order New book/~~Reprint~~*
Date: 22 August 2011
To: Ferndale Printers Ltd, Station Road, Eynsham, Oxford OX33 1PJ

**Please bind 2,750 copies** Your quotation D5492/3 dated 12 August 2011 refers

**Author:** Janey Gledhill
**Title:** An Afternoon by the River
**ISBN:** 000-0-00000-000-0
**Impression:** First
**Trimmed page size:** 216 x 138mm (Demy 8vo; portrait); no bleeds
**Extent:** 352 pages
**Cased/~~paperback~~**
**Imposition:** to suit ~~8/16/24/~~32/~~64~~pp sections
**Binding style:** sewn/~~notched/perfect~~ bound/
rounded and backed/~~flat backed/tight backed~~
~~cover scored and glued to spine + 3mm to first and last pages~~
**Endpapers:** Front and back: 135gsm cartridge; you to print 1/0 (PMS 1795U) from PDF we will supply
**Illustrations:** 00 ~~pages of plates to appear as wraps/inserts between the following pages~~
**Lining:** single
**Head and tail bands:** Bowden's 333 (red, white and blue)
**Cloth:** Wibalin Buckram 563 (dark blue)
**Board:** 1300gsm binder's board
**Blocking:** on spine only in imitation gold foil
**Brasses:** you to supply from artwork we will provide
**Trimming:** all round/~~flush/top and foredge/uncut~~
**Edges:** plain/~~coloured/gilded/~~
~~top/foredge/~~all round
**Jacket/cover:** pre-printed jackets/~~covers~~ with you/~~to be supplied from~~
**Delivery:** Please send 3 advance copies by 21 September 2011 to Lizzie Yates at the above address for approval before stock is delivered to our warehouse.

On approval of advance copies, please deliver 2,747 (or balance) copies to our warehouse:

87 Stockton Way,
Northampton NN2 3BG

Please note that stock will only be accepted by the warehouse once notification of approval of advance copy has been received by them.

*Special instructions*

Advice notes are to be provided in duplicate. They should not be included with the stock, but should be sent separately with the driver. Both copies are to be signed by the person receiving stock, and one copy is to be sent back to the supplier.

Deliveries to the warehouse must be arranged with the warehouse prior to dispatch of stock. Please telephone the Incoming Goods Department on 01604 576132 to make the necessary arrangements.

Where deliveries are made on pallets, they must conform to the following specification:

- 1000 x 1200mm, 4-way entry, non-reversible Europallet
- Maximum height, including pallet, is 1220mm
- Maximum weight is 1 tonne
- Parcels on the pallet must be stacked at least 50mm in from the edge all round

Parcels should conform to the following specification:

- Maximum length from front to back 406mm
- Maximum weight 13.5 kg

Signed
Lizzie Yates
(Production Controller)

---

The information about head bands, cloth and endpapers is now specific. The maker's name and the reference number for blue and gold head bands replace the necessarily vague reference to them in the specification. The same is true of the endpapers which now have a specific PMS colour, and of the imitation cloth. I should point out that the names of the suppliers of the head and tail bands and the imitation cloth are for the ones which would have been used for the job. Obviously, there are other sources for case material and head and tail bands.

The procedural information is very important, and suppliers should be aware that they need to follow it to the letter to avoid the risk of problems occurring at the last moment – for example, stock being delivered to the warehouse without prior arrangement and having to be turned away and sent back to the supplier; or pallets that cannot be stacked on the warehouse racking because they have been loaded too high, both of which cause delay and cost money to sort out.

## The cover/jacket printing and finishing order

The final production order is the cover/jacket printing and finishing order which typically contains the information below.

---

We will supply you with a PDF of the jacket. You to print 5/0 (CMYK + PMS) on a 125gsm single-sided art; matt laminate using 12 micron OPP laminate; spot UV varnish [refer back to Chapter 2 for full details]. Jacket bleeds.

---

### CHARLES BRAND PUBLISHING

14 Headington Avenue, Headington, Oxford OX3 8AB
Phone: +44 (0)1865 971885
Mobile: +44 (0)774 501 6654
Email: cbrandpublishing@oxfordpublishing.com

*~~Cover~~/jacket printing and finishing order*
*New book/~~Reprint~~*

Date: 22 August 2011
To: Ferndale Printers Ltd, Station Road, Eynsham, Oxford OX33 1PJ

**Please print 2,750\* ~~covers~~/jackets** Your quotation D5492/3 dated 12 August 2011 refers

(\*Quantity should include surface finish and binding spoilage, so that there are enough copies to complete binding)

**Author:** Janey Gledhill
**Title:** An Afternoon by the River
**ISBN:** 000-0-00000-000-0
**Impression:** First

**Trimmed page size:** 216 × 138mm (Demy 8vo; portrait); no bleeds
**Cased/~~paperback~~**
**Process:** offset litho: 5/0 CMYK + PMS 296C. From PDF supplied with application file.
**Finish:** 12 micron OPP matt lamination with spot UV varnish.
**Jacket paper:** 125gsm single-sided art
On completion of printing, please send jackets to bindery.

Signed
Lizzie Yates
(Production Controller)

The only points to make here are that:

- the quantity needs to be flexible to take into account the customs of the trade by which the supplier is entitled to deliver up to 10 per cent more copies than ordered, and the possibility that the promotions and publicity department will ask for extra copies for promotional purposes.
- the application file is being supplied with the PDF file so that the printer can access the design and, if necessary, adjust the spine width on the cover/jacket to produce an exact fit without having to go back to the publisher. In the case of this book, the supplier had given the spine widths to production, who had passed them on to the designer. Nevertheless, it is a procedural requirement in the company that all jacket/cover PDF files must be accompanied by the relevant application file.

## Managing the project

With the issuing of the production orders, the job goes live, and production now focuses on:

- maintaining the relationship with the supplier
- following the job through by:

  o monitoring the progress of the project during printing, binding and delivery
  o controlling and dealing with any problems or delays.

### *Maintaining the relationship with the supplier:*
### *monitoring and controlling progress*

Although the supplier's representative still calls on production on a regular basis looking for more work and occasionally dealing with problems, the day-to-day operational running of the job is handled by the supplier's account executive working in the factory, and it is with the account executive that production discusses progress, as well as any problems, and the best way to solve them. The account executive is production's main point of contact with the factory, and it is essential for both parties to get on well with, and trust, each other. The account executive is there to work for their client and to make the experience of producing books with their company as pleasant, positive and stress-free as possible. Where this doesn't happen, the supplier should put another account executive to work with production.

Two of the most important aspects of following a job through are communication and monitoring what is going on in terms of progress (time) and quality.

### Communication

Issuing production orders is the start of the manufacturing process, not the end, and once the job has started you should be in frequent contact with the account executive to check progress against the schedule. Rather than wait for something to arrive, and being surprised when it doesn't arrive as scheduled, it is better to get in touch with the account executive to find out, for example, if the running sheets scheduled for delivery three days hence are likely to arrive. Being proactive and ahead of the game is preferable to being reactive and constantly struggling to get things back on track, or explaining to the editor why something needed urgently hasn't arrived, and won't do so for another three days. Beware of supplier silence, it can often be a sign that something is going wrong. By regularly keeping in touch with the account executive, you have a greater chance of finding out when something goes wrong, and a greater chance of putting it right when it is still a relatively small problem.

### Monitoring quality

Throughout the manufacturing process, there are opportunities to check the quality of the output from one process before it becomes the input for the next:

- proofs
- running sheets
- sample cases
- advance copies.

Although some publishers have decided that they will not check quality, maintaining that this is the responsibility of the supplier, these are useful points at which to detect any problems, especially if they are detected early on. However, as the project advances there is a law of diminishing returns, when the only consolation of finding out at advance copy stage that 10,000 copies of a perfect bound paperback have been given the wrong version of the cover is that they weren't dispatched to the warehouse, and didn't make it into the bookshops.

What to look for when you check quality is discussed in the relevant chapters on printing and binding.

Although the quality you asked for is the quality you should get, there are times when it is necessary to see final quality in relation to its fitness for purpose rather than as an absolute. This is more an argument for pragmatism than relativism, or the attitude that anything goes. But there are occasions when accepting a small defect, and a credit note from the supplier, may be preferable to reprinting or rebinding the entire job.

### What do you do when things go wrong?

However carefully a project is planned, and however carefully it is monitored, there is always the possibility that the unexpected will happen and throw the project off schedule, or make it necessary to rework some of the printing or binding. The first thing to do is to assess the situation, and this is done by establishing what has happened, the extent of the problem, and its likely effect on the project. This will most certainly involve talking to the account executive and to in-house colleagues, who may well come up with ideas for workable solutions.

It is important to move quickly to prevent the problem from escalating, and to have remedies in place as soon as possible. It's only when the problem has been solved and the project is moving forward again – and only then – that you can start to work out what went wrong, how it went wrong, whose fault it is, how to prevent it recurring, and the amount of compensation you could reasonably expect, if the supplier is at fault. Remember that the person whose fault it might be could well be the person most able to sort out the problem.

Being able to sort out problems depends to quite a large extent on a good knowledge of:

- the project and its schedule
- raw materials
- production and manufacturing processes.

It also depends a lot on interpersonal skills, and one's ability to motivate people when the going gets tough. The more you know the less difficult it is. The case study below shows how a problem was successfully dealt with.

### Case study 3.1

This case study involves the simultaneous publication of 1,000 copies each of three books as a mini series. The cover proofs of each book were checked by the editor, the designer and the author, and then passed for press. The books were printed, and running sheets of the text and the covers were submitted for approval before binding started.

Two of the books were fine, but on the cover of the third book, the production controller discovered that while the title on the title page inside the book, as well as the running head at the top of every page, appeared as *The Journey to Jerusalem – and beyond*, the title on the front panel, spine and back panel of the cover appeared as *Journey to Jerusalem – and beyond*.

Since binding was not allowed to start until approval of the running sheets had been received, none of the books had been bound, and so all that needed to be done was to print a new cover. However, because the supplier wanted to bind all three books at the same time (and a competitive quote had been submitted on this basis), the time needed to print a new cover, without which binding couldn't start, would slow the entire job down to the point of not having stock ready in time for the publication date.

While the publisher was deciding what action to take:

- the printer was asked to have a time slot and a press available to print the cover
- the designer was contacted, and asked to supply a fresh PDF file with the correct title, and this was done immediately.

As it turned out, the publisher and the author decided against printing a new cover, deciding instead that the problem was not significant enough to incur the extra cost of printing and relaminating a new cover, or to delay publication; and the correct cover could be substituted when the book was reprinted.

Because the problem was spotted fairly early on (though, in fact, it should have been spotted even earlier – at proof stage) the knock-on effects were minimal, and the books were published as scheduled. This would not have been the case had the publisher decided that a new cover needed to be printed; or, worse still, if the books had been bound, and the problem was discovered then. If that had happened, the only option would have been to pulp all 1,000 defective books, and do a reprint.

## Bringing the project to a close

The point at which bound stock is accepted by the warehouse can be taken as the point at which production's responsibility for the project ends. From now on the books are the responsibility of the warehouse, of sales and marketing, and the commissioning editor. The next time production is involved with this book is when it is to be reprinted, or when it is published as a new edition.

Although production is no longer responsible for the books, there are still several tasks connected with the project that need to be completed before it can be brought to a close.

## Checking suppliers' invoices

The first is to check suppliers' invoices against the estimate, and approve them. Where the price tallies exactly with what was quoted, there should be no problem in approving them, and passing them on to whomever is responsible for arranging payment. However, if the costs in the invoice differ from those appearing in the estimate it is important to establish why this should be so, as price variation may be for a number of reasons:

- changes to the original specification; though in this case, it is usual for the printer to be asked to provide a fresh estimate
- the estimate is no longer valid (estimates are often valid for a given period, usually 30 days, after they have been submitted)
- rises in the price of raw materials and labour; though it is customary for the printer to make sure that clients are aware of these
- fewer or more copies were delivered than ordered (variations in quantity are allowed under the printer's standard conditions of contract, unless agreed otherwise).

Once you are satisfied that there are valid reasons for the variation in price, the invoice can be approved for payment. But, if you are not satisfied with the reasons, the invoice should be returned to the printer with an explanation of why it is being returned, and a request for it to be adjusted to reflect what you expected to pay.

Fortunately, this situation seldom occurs. However, when it does it is important that it should be solved quickly and transparently, thus removing any temptation on the part of the supplier to add a little bit here and a little bit there, and thereby nibbling away at the publisher's profitability.

If the difference cannot be resolved by discussion and negotiation, the next step is arbitration, in which both parties agree to submit their differences to an impartial referee chosen by them, and usually drawn from the industry. This is most often the point of last resort, and fortunately has only occurred once in my experience. It is, however, preferable to taking the dispute to court, which while it ultimately and inevitably produces a verdict, can be expensive and time consuming.

## Archiving information

The next task is to go through the files to make sure that there is enough relevant information for someone, who was not necessarily involved with the project, to be able to produce a reprint without needing to go back to the original project team.

The most useful documents are:

- the latest version of the specification and request for estimate
- the latest supplier's quotations and in-house estimate workings
- all production orders
- any comments on specific problems or on matters that should be known about by the next person working on the book.

### Reflecting on the project: lessons learned

It is precisely because life in production can be so relentlessly hectic and busy, and there is a tendency to move without thinking from one project to another, that reflection plays such a vital part in project management, and why reflection should be formalised to become standard procedure at the end of a project, giving everyone involved a chance to discuss what they think went well, what didn't go well and how things can be done better the next time. Reflection should take no longer than 20–30 minutes, especially if project team members know that it is standard, and come to the meeting prepared.

The aim of reflection is to:

- assess how well the project went
- identify what mistakes or problems (if any) affected it, and why
- develop a strategy for avoiding a recurrence of those mistakes and problems
- identify and consolidate good practice.

The time taken to reflect is well spent, and for the person armed with the understanding that comes from it, with a strategy they are willing to put into operation, the next project should be easier to plan and run.

Most books on project management contain at some point two quotations, both of which emphasise the importance of reflection and learning from it. The first comes from the Chinese philosopher Confucius (551–479 BCE):

> By three methods we may learn wisdom:
> The first, by reflection, which is noblest;
> The second, by imitation, which is easiest;
> The third by experience, which is the bitterest.

The second is from the Spanish philosopher George Santayana (1863–1952):

> Those who cannot remember the past are condemned to repeat it.

We have now come to the end of this section which has concentrated on the strategic and operational aspects of project and production management. In the sections that follow, the focus is on processes and raw materials, and production's involvement and relationship to them as the project develops from a collection of digital files into bound copies of a book in the warehouse.

# 4 Prepress

In this chapter we are concerned with the processes of taking the author's content to the point that it can either follow one route and become a printed book, or another route and become an electronic product appearing in a number of formats, which may include apps for mobile devices, ebooks and web pages.

We start the chapter by looking at the different workflows publishers use to take content (which includes text as well as images) from its initial state as a Word document through a series of editorial and design processes to the point that it is ready to be transformed into a printed book or an electronic product.

From there we look at how images are handled, proofing and Job Definition Format (JDF) before ending the chapter with an exploration of the production department's involvement in all these areas.

## Workflows

Workflow is a term used to describe the route taken by content as it moves through the publishing processes, and can include:

- writing (or authoring)
- editing, which includes desk- and copy-editing
- design and layout
- composition (also known as typesetting) and styling.

The biggest single difference between workflow today and workflow, say, twenty years ago, is that everything is now digital. Content is digital: the words that make up the text, the photographs, the maps, the line drawings; and the processes used to create, design, transmit and store it are also digital. However, while the workflows that we shall be looking at are all digital, there are distinguishing features that make them more or less suitable for a particular context, as we shall see.

There are enormous advantages that come with doing things digitally. It is easy to create content and to move it around within and between documents, in ways that would have been inconceivable when text was created using a typewriter. Images, now that they are digital, can be inserted into text in any position wanted, which would not have been possible when images were mounted on wooden blocks. Documents can be transmitted between author and publisher using email so that distance and time are now no longer limiting factors. The author's keystrokes can now be harnessed to drive film setters or image setters, making double keystroking a thing of the past. In short: digital is everywhere, and everything is digital.

However, as already mentioned, there are different approaches to the use of digital workflows, which depend on a number of factors. Basically, workflows can be divided into three broad types:

- traditional (or conventional)
- XML workflow
- hybrid.

Let's now look at these workflows in more detail. For the sake of simplicity, we shall look at the workflows from a text-only perspective, leaving images until later in the chapter.

## Traditional, or conventional, workflow

The traditional, or conventional, workflow is still very widely used by publishers in the UK and elsewhere, most usually when the final product is intended to appear in print only.

In this workflow, the author's manuscript arrives at the publisher in any number of formats: disc, memory stick, email or hard copy. If it has been typewritten (which is rare, but not unheard of), it is not, therefore, in a digital form, and cannot be used in the workflow, until it has been converted, which can either be done by rekeying, scanning for facsimile output or OCR reading from a scanned copy.

Once the work has been accepted for publication, it goes to content editing and then to copy-editing, where the copy-editor works on the text to ensure that it follows house style, and is consistent and accurate.

At the same time the text is prepared for composition (or typesetting) by marking up the various elements in it which give it its structure – for example, chapter headings, paragraph headings, subheadings. This is done using a set of codes which identify these elements, and make it possible for the designer to specify how they should be treated typographically (and therefore visually) in terms of their positioning (ranged left, centred, etc.), typeface, size and font in such a way as to:

- signal to the reader the different levels of importance (or hierarchy) of the various elements in the text – for example, part headings are considered more important than chapter headings, which are considered more important than subheadings, all of which needs to be transmitted typographically
- distinguish elements from each other
- reflect the relationship of the elements to each other.

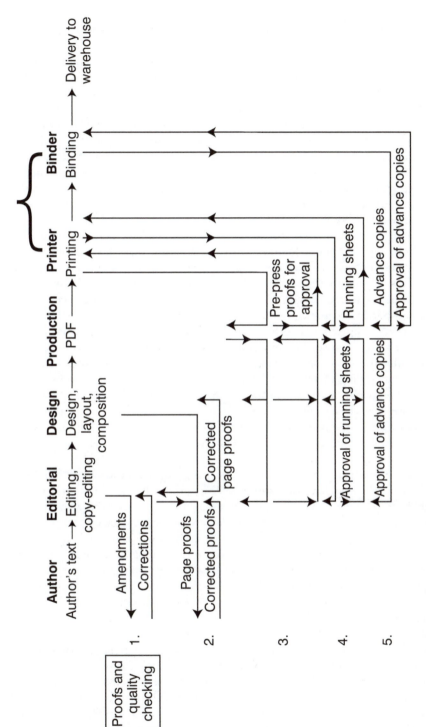

*Figure 4.1* A conventional publishing workflow process

The hierarchy of headings and subheadings may also be used in the creation of a table of contents (TOC).

So, in a novel the structure could be quite simple, and be limited to one or two elements: a chapter number, or a chapter number and title. Whereas in a biography, the structure is likely to be more complex with a host of different elements such as (in addition to chapter numbers and titles), epigraphs, extracts, quotations, footnotes, as well as a range of headings and subheadings, all of which need to be coded so that they can be properly treated.

It is quite possible that the publisher may have created a set of design templates for the copy-editor to work from, rather than expecting them to come up with everything from scratch. Templates do make the copy-editor's work easier and more efficient, even though they may not exactly match, or deal with, the way the text has been structured by the author.

It might be thought that the author would be the best person to code the text, since they are more familiar with its structure than anyone else. While this may be the case, it does not often happen in practice – at the moment at least. This is partly because the author is more taken up with thinking about and writing the text than with how to structure it at anything more than a basic level; and partly because being able to do this properly does require a reasonable level of competence, which the copy-editor is more likely to have than the author, mainly because the copy-editor does this kind of work on a regular basis, and is not involved in trying to create content at the same time as writing it down and styling it. However, there are some authors, who, as we shall see later, are prepared, and able, to format their own text if by doing so they can make sure that their book is published quicker, and earlier than if this work had been done by the publisher. These are most often professional authors working in scientific, technical and medical publishing, and writing about time-sensitive issues, where speed is critical.

Once the text has been copy-edited and designed, it is ready to be output as proofs. Before the advent of desktop publishing, the only way this could be done would be to send marked-up copy to a professional typesetter, who would typeset the text, and supply proofs – either as galley proofs, page on galley proofs (where text is divided into pages, but is minus running heads and page numbers), or page proofs (text is divided into pages, complete with running heads and page numbers). Today, this work can be done either by a designer using a design application like InDesign or QuarkXPress, or by a professional typesetter. Whichever option is preferred, proofs need to be produced so that the author, editor and designer can check that they have been set accurately, that content makes sense, and that the design has worked. Once read, the proofs are returned for correction. Further proofs are produced, read and returned for correction in an iterative process which continues until such time as the text is considered ready for press.

Some authors and editors take advantage of the fact that text is digital, and prefer to receive and return proofs electronically, reading them on screen, and marking any changes or corrections through annotations to the file. Doing things this way certainly speeds up the process as:

- there are no parcels to be packed up and sent off
- delivery is instant
- it is as easy to send proofs to one author as it is to a dozen
- proofs don't get lost in the post.

All of which contributes to making life in the production department simpler and easier, particularly when a project may have multiple authors, or you could be working on several different projects at once.

As mentioned, proofing continues with one set of revises following another until such time as the editor and author are both satisfied that the work has reached a point at which it can be passed for press.

While this happens you should be monitoring progress to make sure that things are moving according to schedule.

If the typesetting has been done by the supplier who is going to do the printing, all that need be done is to instruct them to proceed with printing and binding once everything has been passed for press; and this is usually done by issuing a printing and a binding order.

If the typesetting has been done by, say, a designer or a trade supplier, you need to arrange for the work to be transferred to the printer. This is most usually done by email or by using a web-based file transfer protocol (FTP). Where this is not feasible, for one reason or another, it is still possible to transfer work on a disc, though this is far from ideal, as you will find it difficult to work easily with the supplier who doesn't have email facilities.

If you are sending work to a supplier it is still quite common practice to ask for some form of proof so that you can check that the file transfer has been successful. However, as discussed, this is not always done. With the approval of the proof, the traditional prepress workflow has now finished. The next stage is printing and binding.

## File transfer

File transfer can be done by email, disc or FTP. When you transfer files to a supplier, it is really important to let the printer know that you are planning to do this and, once you have sent the file off, to check with the printer that it has been successfully received. Assuming that successful transfer is always the case, and not carrying out this simple check, can lead to unexpected and unwelcome delays. The most commonly used format is the print-ready, printed-page format, Portable Document Format file, more usually known as a PDF. Developed and maintained by Adobe Systems, it is now the *de facto* industry standard for file transfer, though it is equally possible (though not considered as convenient) to submit text in native production (or application) files, such as InDesign or QuarkXPress.

## The Portable Document Format file (PDF)

The PDF provides two functions: first of all, digital files can now be submitted to the printer that are completely independent of the hardware, software or operating systems used to create them, and of the devices which are going to be used to output them. To those who have grown up using PDFs this may not seem particularly remarkable, but for those who were working in the pre-PDF era, the freedom of choice that comes with using PDFs is a real advantage – a job is now no longer bound by considerations of who created it or how, or whether it is going to be compatible with the equipment to be used to reproduce it. So, this means that you can now send the same PDF to a printer working in the Far East as to one working in the USA, without having to make sure that either printer is able to handle it. This function is, of course, at the heart of distributed printing, making it possible to print stock simultaneously in different parts of the world, using different printing technologies, as discussed in Chapter 6 on printing.

The second function of the PDF is to check the integrity of the content (text as well as graphics) before it is submitted to the printer. This process is known as preflight, or preflighting, and its purpose is to pick up and identify any problems that would make the content otherwise unusable by the printer, and cause delay while the problem was being sorted out. The most common problems are to do with missing or substituted fonts, and missing graphics files, even though these are supposed to be embedded in the PDF.

### Preflighting

Although preflighting is done in-house and is now part of the process of creating a PDF file, the printer will also carry out their own preflight checks to make sure that everything works at their end.

If something does go wrong when the printer is preflighting the publisher's file, it is common practice for the publisher to put things right, rather than asking, or expecting, the printer to do this: mainly because it is easier for the publisher to do so, as they have access to the original files, and should know what to do to correct the problem; but it also makes it completely clear where responsibility lies if subsequent problems occur.

The one exception to this practice is with jacket and cover printing, where the PDF is submitted with the application file – that is, the file containing the pre-PDF data. Having the application file to hand gives the printer instant access to the artwork if adjustments are needed to the jacket or cover artwork, which in most cases involves playing with the spine width. Without the application file, the printer has to go back to the publisher to get them to make the adjustments. This takes time, and adjustments may not be as accurate as they might have been had the printer been able to make them.

### XML workflows

At the other end of the spectrum to the traditional, or conventional, workflow lie the XML workflows. The acronym XML stands for Extensible Markup Language, and XML is a descendant of an earlier markup language SGML (which stands for Standard Generalized Markup Language), and closely related

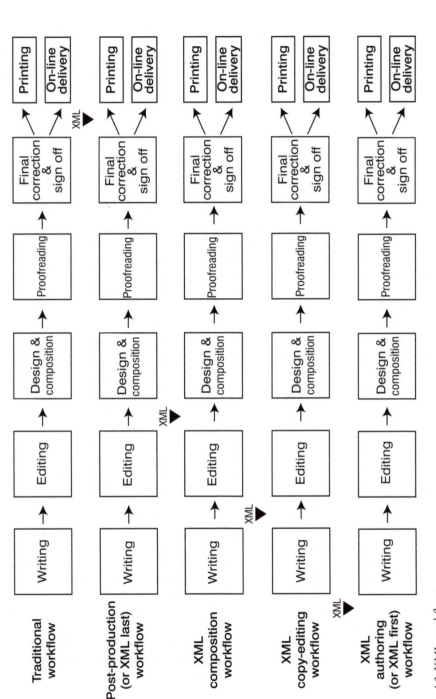

*Figure 4.2* XML workflows

to HTML, which stands for Hypertext Markup Language. Markup languages were created so that the structure and meaning of content can be separated from its style (or the way it looks). Doing this makes it possible to use content in ways that would not be possible if content were left in its undifferentiated digital form, as is the case with the traditional workflow. To appreciate what this means we need first to understand the nature of content.

### The nature of digital content

Content used in the traditional workflow, although it is digital, is virtually inert, and doesn't lend itself readily to appearing in the flexible and dynamic world of electronic publishing. One of the reasons for this is that although un-marked-up content can be *read* by a computer, it cannot be *understood* – the computer is unable to give any meaning to the elements it comes across, and is therefore unable to do anything with them.

As an example, let's look at the use of italics, and how, although they all *look* alike, they can be used for different purposes, and to convey different meanings:

- emphasis and stress
- highlighting
- foreign words and phrases
- titles of books, newspapers, magazines, etc.
- stage directions in plays
- introducing cross-references
- lists
- names of ships, aeroplanes and vehicles
- names of plaintiff and defendant in legal cases
- biological names and classifications
- mathematics.

For the copy-editor, working in a traditional workflow, it is enough to mark each occurrence of any of the above as italic for them to be set in italic. There is no need to define the sense in which the italic is being used – italic is italic is italic. There is no chance of ambiguity or confusion because, to the reader, the context is sufficiently clear to make the meaning obvious. For example, in a legal report it is enough to know that in the heading *Queen of Hearts* v. *Knave of Hearts*, the italic name on the left is the person bringing the case (the plaintiff), and on the right the defendant. The names cannot be mistaken for a cross-reference or the name of a ship.

However, when it comes to electronic publishing, content is no longer just the words as they appear on the page; content has now become data which can be read and understood by a computer, and can be:

- linked
- referenced

- sorted
- searched for (and on)
- amalgamated
- counted
- indexed
- listed
- re-used, re-versioned, re-purposed and much, much more.

But this can only happen if the computer is able to distinguish and then understand the different elements that appear in the content. Each element needs to be given a semantic meaning which defines what it is, and how it is being used: a book title needs to be defined as being a book title, as opposed to a magazine or journal title. Plaintiffs need to be differentiated from defendants, and ships from plants. Italics alone are no longer enough.

### Markup languages

This is where markup languages come in. Each element is tagged to give it a specific meaning, so that it can be told apart as well as in its relation to other elements. As an example, by tagging the Queen of Hearts as a plaintiff, and tagging the Knave of Hearts as a defendant, a computer can now tell these apart. This would have been impossible if the names had not been tagged at all, or had not been tagged differently. Armed with this kind of information, a computer can now work its way through a law report and produce two separate lists: one showing the names of all the plaintiffs; and the other the names of all the defendants.

However, markup languages are used by publishers for much more than simply creating lists and databases. Using a markup language like XML makes it possible to create files that, because they are language and platform neutral, can be used in any text-based system available now or in the future. The effect of this is that content – and, by extension, intellectual property – can be future-proofed.

By using XML publishers can unleash the power latent in content, through:

- publishing in ebook formats
- creating new products and revenue streams.

In addition, XML can be used to add metadata to content to provide the link between content creator and end-user, and to improve discoverability; and XML data can be stored and edited in a content management system (CMS), for extraction and re-use in different contexts – for example, in reference and catalogues where publications may need to show a subset of the data held by the publisher. Imagine a data set that holds thousands of recipes from all over the world. If these recipes are tagged with the name of the country of origin, it is quite possible to produce a new book containing recipes from individual countries. In much the same way as it would be possible to produce a book of vegetarian recipes from recipes that had been tagged as vegetarian.

## Defining structure through XML document type definitions (DTDs), and schemas

As described above, structure and meaning need to be separated from appearance or style, and this is done through tagging elements to make them explicit and understandable to the computer when it reads through the document.

However, the tags used to mark the various elements in the content have no value on their own. They need to be listed and their relationship to each other defined – a process known as *parsing* – and this is done through the *document type definition* (DTD), which appears at the start of a document as the *document type declaration*. To take an analogy, tags are like words in a language, and the DTD is the grammar which glues the words together, and makes it possible to string them together in a structured and meaningful way, so that we can communicate intelligibly. Without a DTD the document cannot be read and understood.

A schema performs the same role as the DTD, but it is a more powerful alternative, and using a schema makes creating and implementing the grammar easier and more straightforward.

## Styling the appearance of content

The structure and meaning of content are likely to remain more or less unchanged during its lifetime, even though it may appear and reappear several times in different media. However, its appearance and style can be subject to constant and dramatic change as it moves from printed book, to ebook, to computer screen. For example, the printed version of a two-column page in a 279 × 216mm book (Demy 4to) cannot physically be accommodated on the screen of a mobile phone, or an ereader or tablet. It needs to be reformatted so that it can be reflowed. It is for this reason that content in an XML workflow is kept typographically neutral, and only given value, or meaning, just before it is transformed into the end product. This is done through the use of style sheets which, linked to the DTD related to that specific content, describe how the document is to be displayed: the original two columns in the print version are reformatted so that they can appear as a single column on an ereader screen, and as a single column reversed out of a bright-blue rectangle on the web.

## Who uses XML workflows?

Early adopters of XML were scientific, technical and medical (STM), legal, professional and journals publishers, who quickly appreciated the benefits of using XML to create and manage their kind of content, for example:

- online journals
- reference books
- law reports

- dictionaries
- textbooks
- directories
- encyclopaedias.

*Why use an XML workflow?*

Despite a fairly large investment of time up-front, these publishers use XML workflows because they enable them to:

- reduce the time it takes to publish by automating some processes
- reduce the cost of publishing
- develop content simultaneously for use across a range of delivery channels
- re-purpose and re-use content.

However, take-up by the rest of the industry – broadly speaking, trade, academic and educational – has, until recently, been less rapid and less universal, though publishers are now starting to consider the possibility of using an XML workflow, as e-publishing technology becomes more sophisticated and the e-publishing market begins to show signs of growth. But, as we shall see later, there are other routes which can be taken to produce content for e-publishing.

*XML workflows*

As can be seen in Figure 4.2 on p. 83, XML can be introduced into the workflow at a number of different points in the prepress cycle:

- after the print files have been passed for press (post-production, or XML last, also known as back conversion)
- after authoring and editing have been completed (XML composition)
- after authoring (XML copy-editing)
- at the start of the prepress cycle (XML authoring).

Quite where XML is introduced depends on a number of factors, which include skills, resources, time and money, which we shall now look at.

*Post-production XML, or XML last, workflow*

The post-production XML workflow is effectively identical to the conventional workflow, with XML being introduced once everything has been passed for press. The process involves taking post-production inputs which can include printed books (in which case they will need either to be scanned and OCR read or rekeyed) as well as:

- application files
- print-ready PDFs
- electronic files

extracting their content, tagging it, parsing it according to an agreed DTD or schema, and converting it to an XML file which can then be used to produce a number of different formats – electronic as well as physical – with the potential of reaching as wide a range of delivery channels as possible – something not possible if content had remained in print form only.

To avoid confusion, when it comes to scanning already printed books, there is a big difference between scanned content which has been tagged for XML, and content that has been scanned just for print. The latter is only a digital image of the page and, as such, is only capable of producing a facsimile of the original page in the book. If you want to use scanned content for epublishing you will need to remove line endings, which are fixed, to allow content to reflow.

The XML-last workflow is quite widely used: it allows a publisher relatively cheap and easy access to epublishing channels, with the minimum disruption to the existing conventional workflow; and converting content to XML, which is generally quite complex, resource- and labour-intensive work, can be done by an outside supplier who has the necessary skills and equipment.

But, there are limitations to using this workflow, the main one being that a publisher cannot immediately benefit from any advantage that may come with using an XML workflow, having to wait for this until after conversion has been successfully completed.

### The XML composition workflow

In the XML composition workflow XML is introduced to content *after* it has been edited, and *before* it goes for composition or typesetting, so that it becomes an input to the typesetting process. It is quite common for publishers to outsource tagging and typesetting to specialist companies, who carry out the work using DTDs or schemas specially created by them for their clients. XML tagging can also happen through a content management system (CMS) online. This has the added benefit of allowing editing by several people (authors, editors) working on the project at the same time.

Proofs can be read and corrected either on paper, in the PDF, or directly in the XML file (expertise in using XML is not necessary for this).

The XML composition workflow is quite widely used by publishers, aware of the benefits of using XML in terms of cost, time and efficiency (mainly through automation), and the fact that the print file and the XML file are available at the same time, increasing their ability to work on several fronts at once to bring their products to market.

### The XML copy-editing workflow

In this workflow the copy-editor has two options. The first is to do the copy-editing in the Word file, submitted by the author, and to tag content as work proceeds. The tagged Word file is then converted into a format from which it can be typeset, usually by an outside supplier, using the appropriate DTD or schema.

Although this kind of work can be demanding, copy-editors are becoming increasingly confident with it, and the savings in time and cost in this part of the publishing process are quite considerable.

The other option is for the copy-editor to work on a file that has already been converted to XML. Although this is perfectly possible, it does require considerable skill on the part of the copy-editor and the author alike, and would best be done using an online, web-based system, although software tools exist to make the direct editing of XML possible. It should be emphasised, though, that there is a difference in an XML file between displayable content and XML markup, used to define the attributes of the content. These attributes, tags and taxonomy would not be edited.

Proof reading and correction can be done either on paper, in the PDF, or directly in XML.

Again, the advantages for publishers are the same as for other XML workflows.

### *The XML authoring, or XML first, workflow*

This workflow is based on XML throughout, starting with the author producing content in XML (or Word XML), and editing is done onscreen.

This workflow is best suited to authors and copy-editors with experience of XML. For those who are less experienced, producing documents in XML is very demanding, the learning curve for first-time users is steep, and although templates and Word-based authoring tools may help there is always a danger that content produced this way may not be immediately usable.

Nevertheless, where the system works, the advantages of being able to bring products rapidly to market, and the ability to chunk content and produce it across a range of formats and sales channels make this option an attractive one.

### The last word on workflows

As is probably clear by now, one size of workflow does not fit all. Each one has its own merits, and each one requires a different set of skills and resources; and, in turn, each one produces different advantages and benefits for the user.

At the moment the trend in XML-workflow choice appears to be that professional and educational publishers prefer the XML authoring (or XML first) workflow, while academic and journals publishers prefer to use the XML composition workflow.

How long this distinction will last, and how long it will be before trade publishers adopt XML, will depend on two factors:

- growth in the market for electronic products
- alternative ways of developing and producing electronic products.

### Production and XML

Irrespective of where XML is introduced into the workflow, production's involvement is more likely to be confined to managing a workflow than in setting one up. You need to understand how the particular workflow operates, and be able to schedule work passing through the system accordingly.

At the moment the trend is for publishers to send work destined for XML treatment to outside suppliers which specialise in converting content into XML, typesetting it, proofing it, correcting it and creating final output files. These organisations work in XML all day, every day, and are demonstrably a more cost-effective alternative to trying to do XML in-house. Your job in production is to know where to find these organisations and to negotiate a reasonable price and schedule for doing the work.

If you do use outside suppliers an important aspect of your work with XML is archiving, and making sure that the supplier holds the final and most up-to-date version of the content file, and that it is retrievable and usable. Since the whole purpose of XML is to make it possible for a publisher to produce content once and use it many times, it would be difficult, if not impossible, to achieve this if archived material was inaccessible, incomplete or obsolete.

## The hybrid workflow: the easy route to ePub formats

XML has been in use for quite a while now, and when it and the other markup languages were first developed they were seen as the only ways in which content could be treated if it was to appear in other formats besides print.

While today XML is still a very powerful tool ideally suited, as we have seen, to the needs of publishers for creating and producing certain types of content, there are now other ways in which publishers can create e-publishable content without having to engage directly with XML, and which involve nothing more complicated than exporting a file through a design application, like InDesign, straight into an ePub format; though you do need to allow for a bit of tweaking, especially where graphics are concerned.

This is ideal for publishers who only really want to be able to get access to epublishing, and are producing content that does not need all the additional features that come with going down the XML route. Doing it this way is quick, easy to use and above all it is relatively cheap. In addition, it doesn't require specialist knowledge other than what is needed to run a particular design application; and it is virtually immediate because it can be done either in-house, or by the designer, at the same time as they produce the print-ready PDF.

Currently, the most often supported format for ebooks is the ePub standard (see the International Digital Publishing Forum [IDPF]) website, and the files within the ePub package use XML. Although there are software tools to generate ePub files from word-processed text and page layout files, it should be remembered that directly compiling ePub files from XML data may be easier in some situations.

## Images

So far we have concentrated on text. Let's now turn our attention to images (also known as illustrations) and see how they fit into the workflow.

Images – photographs, drawings, paintings – come in all sizes and shapes, and in an assortment of colours: black and white, duotone, polychrome.

They can be submitted in a digital format, and they can be submitted in an analogue format: for example, an original painting, a set of photographic prints, a box of old transparencies or a picture from a 4-colour magazine. Where this happens, the first step is conversion to a digital format. This is usually done by scanning, which would certainly be the case with the photographic prints, the transparencies (though prints could also be made from these, which could then be scanned), and the magazine picture even though it has already been printed and has a screen ruling.

But what happens if the painting is too big to fit onto the scanner, the surface is too rough for the scanner to pick up the detail, or it can't be removed from its frame? The answer is to take a picture, obviously with a digital camera.

### Digital image formats

Some digital formats are better than others, because they are easy to send and receive, they are simple to work with, and they give better finished results, which is particularly important when it comes to 4-colour offset printing. So, the more control you can exercise over the format in which images are submitted, the easier (and better) it is for you.

Image formats for print and archiving are:

- TIFF (Tagged Image File Format) files also known as TIF (if you are working with PCs)
- EPS (Encapsulated PostScript) files
- Duotone EPS files
- DCS (Desktop Color Separations) files
- PDF (Portable Document Format) files
- PSD (Photoshop Document) files
- SVG (Scalable Vector Graphic) files.

Image formats that can be used for screen-based output (web or ebook) are:

- PNG (Portable Network Graphics) files
- GIF (Graphics Interchange Format) files
- JPEG (Joint Photographic Experts Group) files, also known as JPG when using a PC.

These formats are fine for screen viewing, but they cannot be used in offset printing without the extra work and care needed when having to convert them to a more suitable format, which takes time, costs money and is not always error free. In a job with a lot of illustrations, this is something you would want to avoid.

## The JPEG format (also known as JPG in the world of PCs)

The acronym stands for the Joint Photographic Experts Group, which is the name of the standardisation committee which designed the JPEG compression algorithm. JPEG images come in a special class of their own, with their own characteristics, and this makes them unsuitable for offset print reproduction. The two most serious negative characteristics are a JPEG's:

- 'lossiness', which means that it loses image quality (because of data loss) each time it is opened and saved during design
- inability to deal with sharp changes in tone.

So, while it may not be an ideal candidate for print reproduction, it is certainly worth remembering that JPEGs lend themselves well to appearing on a screen.

## Resolutions for photography, scanning and printing

A digital image, for example a photograph taken with a digital camera, is made up of series of small squares, known as pixels (which stands for picture elements), arranged in a matrix of horizontal rows and vertical columns. A photograph taken with a digital camera (or mobile phone, now) is divided into a matrix of horizontal and vertical pixels each of which contributes to the detail of the image. The more pixels there are, the finer the detail, and the bigger the file size. In a digital photograph there may be as many as 6,000,000 pixels (6 megapixels) arranged in 2,000 rows of 3,000 pixels each. In the context of photography, the word resolution describes the number of pixels in that photograph.

To turn these pixels into something which can be used to print from on an offset press, they need first to be scanned to become dots per inch (dpi), and then converted into a screen ruling of lines per inch (lpi).

Before the scanning resolution can be decided there are two factors that need to be taken into account. The first is the size of the image as it is going to appear on the printed page, and the second is the type of paper on which the image is to be printed.

Let's start with size and the scanning resolution. If we take a row of 3,000 pixels (as in the photograph mentioned above) and decide to put them into a picture which is 8 inches (or 20.32cm) wide, each linear inch of the picture will contain 375 pixels, making each pixel just 0.0026 of an inch wide. If we take the same row, and decide to put it into a picture which is 5 inches wide, the amount of pixels per linear inch increases to 600 and, naturally, their size decreases to 0.0017 of an inch so that they can all fit into the space available. So, final size is an important consideration.

The other factor is the paper on which the job is to be printed, which affects the value of the line screen used in converting the image into something that can be used to print from. Coated papers work well with fine screens (120 lines per inch and upwards). Uncoated papers ranging from newsprint to smooth, but uncoated, machine finished (MF) papers work better with screen rulings starting 65 lpi and going up to 120, depending on how absorbent and rough surfaced the paper is.

Screen rulings range from coarse to fine, starting with 65 lines per inch and going up to as many as 200. As a rough guide:

- the coarser the screen the larger the halftone dot, and the less the detail
- the rougher the paper the coarser the screen.

For book work the screen rulings generally start at 120 lpi and go up to 150. For high quality art books, you might choose a finer screen, but for most colour work 150 is fine enough.

Now that we have considered these two factors, what effect do they have on the scanning resolution? As we have already seen, the more pixels there are per inch, the greater the detail. However, since the amount of detail that can be produced depends on the size of the picture and the halftone screen ruling, there is little point in having more detail than can be reproduced. It is simply wasted. As a general rule of thumb, you are advised to scan at about *twice* the amount of the screen ruling. So, if your screen ruling is 150 lpi, you should scan at 300 dpi; a screen ruling of 12 lpi, scan at 240 dpi, and so on.

Most of this work is done by the designer, and in production you are not likely to be involved in all these calculations. Nevertheless, whoever is dealing with images will need to know what kind of paper you are going to print the job on before they start scanning.

Remember, too, that it is always useful to discuss things with the supplier, just to make sure that everyone is working to the same set of parameters to achieve a common goal.

## Proofing and managing quality

Proofing provides the opportunities in the project when the outputs from one process can be checked before they become the inputs for the next one. For text this is relatively easy: the typesetter sets text as instructed, and submits proofs to the publisher who, in turn sends them to the author to read and make sure that their text has been correctly set; to the designer (if one was involved) to check that the design has worked and has been implemented correctly; and finally to production to check the overall quality of the supplier's work. The involvement of this many people looking at the proofs from such different perspectives should effectively eliminate any errors or underlying problems. Production's involvement tends to be focused on things like pagination, running heads, and less on content, this being left to the author and editor. I always make it a practice to do a quick eye-read of every page of every book I deal with. The time, hassle and money I have saved far outweighs the time spent doing it.

Let's start by looking at text-only proofs first, as these are easier than proofs of integrated books, in which text and image share the same page.

Text proofs are usually supplied as page proofs where everything is in position and looks like the final product, which makes it easy to judge type size, typeface, use of space, readability, etc. Proofs can run to several revisions which, if allowed for in the schedule, shouldn't be a problem. Problems arise when the author starts to rewrite the text in proof, because introducing changes, once text has been typeset, costs money and takes time.

This is why most publishers have an author's correction allowance, which allows the author to make corrections up to a certain value, usually expressed as a percentage of the original typesetting cost, after which they will have to bear the cost of corrections themself.

While it is possible to control the rising costs of correction, it is less easy to control the loss of time if people start running late with their proofs. So, as already discussed in the sections on scheduling in Chapter 2, you would be well advised to make an allowance in your schedule for this, especially when you are dealing with multiple authors or a complex project, even if you think it won't happen.

Proofing can be done in two ways: one is to have proofs printed on paper (hard copy); the other is to have them submitted electronically. The hard copy route is really labour intensive and time consuming: proofs have to be made up into sets, packed and sent off. They take time to reach their destination, and because they use paper and may have to travel long distances, their environmental impact can be significant. The advantages of having proofs sent and returned electronically (or digitally) have already been described above. Ironically, the recipient of electronic proofs may choose to print them out, which rather defeats the purpose in the first place, especially if they mark and return their corrections on the hard copy! The more proofing can be done electronically, the better for the environment, and the easier it is to manage the project.

### Prepress proofing of images

Prepress proofing of images allows the designer, the author and the editor to:

- check the quality of the scanning (or origination) in terms of sizing, detail and faithfulness to the original
- judge how well the images work with each other in terms of size and positioning, either as part of a separate plate section, or as integrated images sharing the same page with the text
- to check the quality of the images as they will appear on the printed page.

### Digital proofing

Software is available that makes it easy to scan images and to see the output virtually in real time on a screen, via email as a PDF or over the internet. However, if this is not an option, it is possible to produce printed proofs using a laser printer or an inkjet printer.

Producing proofs for monochrome work is relatively straightforward. However, for colour work, things are slightly more complicated. This is for several reasons, the first of which is that colour looks different when reproduced on different input, display and output devices such as:

- computer screen
- laser printer
- inkjet printer
- offset press.

Some way of managing colour is needed, and this was provided when the International Color Consortium (ICC) introduced their colour management system. This is based on a series of profiles which describe the characteristics of the monitor, the printer and the rendering intents, and make it possible to convert and then transfer colour data between the different colour spaces (RGB for the monitor and CMYK when printed lithographically) of each device, whether these spaces are device dependent (native) or independent. It also makes it possible for information about colour to be moved easily and safely between different computers, operating systems and networks, in ways reminiscent of the flexibility that comes with using a PDF.

In practical terms, using the ICC colour management system means that images can be scanned in one place and printed in another in the certainty that colours that were viewed on the monitor and approved in proof (the inputs) will be predictably and consistently reproduced in the finished product (the output).

### Soft proofing

The ICC colour management system also allows you to view proofs on a computer monitor (soft proofing) safe in the knowledge that what you see is what you will get in terms of what the printed image will look like when it is printed on the paper intended for the job.

There are other advantages that come with soft proofing:

- there are no printed proofs, so you save paper and green your proofing
- you can scan anywhere in the world, and check and correct your proofs in real time
- it is cheap and quick: you don't have to wait for proofs to arrive by post or courier, nor do you have to return them, which would otherwise take time and cost money.

It is for these reasons that soft proofing is now in widespread use.

### Hard proofing: digital proofing

Hard proofing involves producing a printed sample of the finished product on a substrate; and can be either digital or analogue, using a range of devices to produce low- or high-resolution proofs.

Digital device proofs include:

- laser
- inkjet
- dye-sublimation
- plotter.

They also go under a variety of generic and trade names – for example, Matchprint (also spelt Match Print), which is also available in an analogue version.

### Analogue proofing

Analogue proofs take existing film as their starting point, and are printed on paper with the aim of reproducing as closely as possible the look of the finished product. This is possible using the analogue equivalents of digital proofing: for example, Cromalin or Match Prints, although as we will see below, this kind of proofing can only ever be an approximation, and can never match the real thing for authenticity.

In the continuing search for authenticity, it is possible to go a step further and produce proofs on a proofing press, using proper printing inks on the actual paper the job is to be printed on.

But the problem with this kind of proof is that it is unable to replicate exactly the printing conditions of the main production run: proofs taken from a proofing press are printed a colour at a time, and while the press is being washed up for the next colour the ink just printed has time to dry, so that the next layer of ink in the sequence is laid down on ink which is already dry. This proofing is known as wet on dry proofing, whereas the production run is printed wet on wet (wet ink printed immediately onto wet ink) at speeds varying from 12,000 impressions an hour (iph) on a sheet-fed press to 35,000 iph on a web press. Any problems to do with tracking on the main run are unlikely to be shown up in wet on dry proofing.

If the publisher really needs to see what the job will look like on press, they should ask for machine proofs. These proofs are produced on the same machine and paper stock, and at the same speed, as the main run. They are, of course, very expensive to produce; and, in the final analysis, they only serve to show that these proofs are alright, without necessarily making it possible to predict how the job will turn out when finally printed.

One possibility is for publisher and printer to work from a contract proof, a specific set of proofs which both parties consider as best representing the quality required for the job. Contract proofs are much less expensive than machine proofs. The printer uses the information contained on the proof (colour bars, grey scale), and sets up the press to produce results which match the contract proof exactly.

There is evidence to suggest that publishers are now dispensing with colour proofs altogether, and passing the responsibility entirely to the printer for getting things right – and the risk should things go wrong. The publisher's argument is that since everything has already been proofed and approved before the job was sent to the printer (most probably using a PDF), there is no need to proof things all over again. Their view is that the printer should be capable of producing a good quality product, especially if they are ISO 9001 certified. This approach is relatively recent, and is being adopted by publishers: for example, STM publishers, even though colour may well be critical, as in the case of illustrated medical books.

In spite of the fact that there is a strong case to be made for this approach, my own preference, based on experience, is to ask the printer to supply a digital proof, once they have received the PDF. This is because, as mentioned earlier, I like to work through a book, turning each page to give it a quick eye-read and make sure that everything is as it should be. I prefer to work with soft proofs because they speed things up, and they are eco-friendly at the same time.

## The prepress workflow and Job Definition Format (JDF)

Prepress is a process of preparing content for transformation into some form of product, either print on paper, or electronic; it is about choosing a particular workflow, and organising events so that content moves through the system as quickly as possible.

The main role of the production department is more about managing this process than actual involvement in it. There is a significant amount of work, material, people and resources to be pulled together and co-ordinated in a meaningful and productive way; and as a project manager it is your task to set up a schedule which takes into account all aspects of the job, and controls:

- the start and completion of each process
- the arrival and departure of each component in the book, like text and image files, and proofs
- the deployment of people and equipment.

It is your responsibility to make sure that the schedule is workable, and that everyone involved in the project – within the company and outside – knows and understands the schedule as a whole, and the particular part they play in it. It is also your responsibility to monitor the performance of the schedule, and to take timely and appropriate action to prevent things from being delayed or from going wrong thereby damaging the schedule.

To be able to do this effectively, you need to be able to remember:

- what has been done
- what is being done at the moment
- what needs to be done next.

Bearing in mind that you will quite probably be running several projects simultaneously, all of them progressing at different speeds and all at different stages of development, being able to do this requires either a prodigious memory or a system that does it for you.

Apart from various project management packages available to do this, it is worth mentioning the Job Definition Format (JDF), which is gradually attracting attention in the printing industry, as well as the publishing industry.

JDF is an XML-based industry standard, which is being developed by the international consortium CIP4 (the International Co-operation for the Integration of Processes in Prepress, Press and Postpress Organization). According to the CIP4 website, JDF:

- 'is designed to streamline information exchange between different applications and systems
- is intended to enable the entire industry, including media, design, graphic arts, on-demand and e-commerce companies, to implement and work with individual workflow solutions
- will allow integration of heterogeneous products from diverse vendors to create seamless workflow solutions.'

www.cip4.org/overview/what_is_jdf.html

The idea of an entire workflow being linked from publisher through supplier to the finished product through an electronic job ticket is an attractive one, particularly with the increased need for speed to market. As the CIP4 website says, the most prominent features of JDF are its ability to:

- carry a print job from genesis through completion. This includes a detailed description of the creative, prepress, press, postpress and delivery processes
- bridge the communication gap between production and Management Information Services (MIS). This ability enables instantaneous job and device tracking as well as detailed pre- and post-calculation of jobs in the graphic arts
- bridge the gap between the customer's view of product and the manufacturing process by defining a process-independent product view as well as a process-dependent production view of a print job
- define and track any user-defined workflow without constraints on the supported workflow models. This includes serial, parallel, overlapping, and iterative processing in arbitrary combinations and over distributed locations.

www.cip4.org/overview/what_is_jdf.html

JDF is available through Adobe software, and works closely in conjunction with the PDF. An electronic job ticket can be set up at the start of a project so that it travels with the job as it passes through prepress, printing and binding, through to archiving. Used this way, the JDF integrates all aspects of the job from financial such as specification, request for estimate, quotation and final billing, through to logistical in the use of resources, scheduling and communication.

In essence, JDF like any other management system can be used at any point in the publishing cycle to suit the needs of the situation, the project and the people involved. If you are producing only a small number of books in a year, it is quite possible to get by using a system of diary reminders and notes to yourself. If you are producing large quantities of books in different perms and combinations, different formats, different languages in different parts of the globe, then perhaps JDF is the system for you.

Whatever. In the end everything comes down to the quality of your work, and the pleasure (and implicitly the efficiency and effectiveness) with which you carry it out; and this is going to depend on how well you have planned, organised, implemented, monitored and controlled the prepress workflow, and the many strands it contains.

# Part II

# Processes and raw materials

# 5 Raw materials

In this chapter we shall be exploring the raw materials used to create your book:

- paper
- inks
- adhesives
- coatings: lamination and varnishes
- coverings: cloth – real and imitation.

Paper is by far the biggest single component in any print job, and the greater part of the chapter is devoted to it, looking at:

- how it is made
- its properties and how these affect performance and suitability
- the various types of paper you can choose from
- paper defects
- calculating paper quantities for sheet-fed and web-fed jobs
- green and environmental issues.

You might wonder why ink should be included here when, basically, ink is ink. This might have been true twenty years ago, but there is an increased awareness of environmental and health issues associated with certain types of ink, and choices are now available, which need to be understood.

Glues, or adhesives, play a crucial role in joining and holding your product together. Again, there are a lot of glues available – such as hot-melt, cold-melt and PUR – all based on different chemistries, whose properties affect:

- their drying characteristics
- the strength with which they bond to paper and card
- how well they keep their shape.

At the end of the chapter come varnishes, laminates and cloths – real and imitation – all of which may seem small when compared with paper, but are just as important in making sure that your product looks good, and is fit enough for whatever its intended purpose may be.

## Paper

So, let's start with paper.

Unless you are a large publishing company that buys its own paper and supplies it to the printer, you will most probably ask the printer to supply the paper for the job; and more often than not this will be a paper they have in stock, and use frequently.

Doing this has several advantages:

- you don't need to buy paper in advance
- the right quantity of paper is available at the right time and in the right place, and running short is unlikely
- paper is available for short runs and reprints
- the printer is familiar with regularly used stock
- the printer has to sort out any problems
- paper costs are back-loaded, so they are paid only when the job has been completed, which, if your credit terms are good, can be up to 30 or 60 days after the printer submits their invoice.

There are also some disadvantages:

- paper is likely to be more expensive, since the printer has to pay the costs up front, and subsidise your credit period
- choice is limited to what the printer has in stock.

But, on balance, the advantages outweigh the disadvantages,

If you buy paper from the printer, it's common practice for them to discuss the nature of the job with you and build up an understanding of what you are trying to achieve. This makes it easier for them to come up with suggestions on things like weight, bulk, or finish.

Whether you are buying your paper from the printer, or having it made for you by the mill, it is always useful to know about paper in many, if not all, its aspects, if only to be able to talk about it with the printer, or the mill, and make sure you get the paper that's best for the job.

### *The wood*

Since the second half of the nineteenth century the main source of the basic ingredient in paper making – pulp – has been trees, and the best of these are the coniferous, or softwood, trees that are grown in the northern hemisphere – Canada, Scandinavia, Russia and China – such as spruce, pine, fir and larch all of which grow relatively quickly, and produce the long fibres needed for paper making. Some hardwood (or broadleaved) trees such as eucalyptus, aspen and birch are also used, though less extensively.

The tree is felled, and its branches are removed before it is taken to the pulp mill, where large rotary saws cut it into logs about eight feet long (just under

2.5 metres). The logs are put into a debarking drum, where the bark is removed. The debarked logs are now ready to be turned into the pulp, the first step on their journey to becoming paper.

### The pulp

Turning logs into pulp can be done in several ways, each of which produces a different quality pulp as a result, which in turn is used to produce different grades of paper.

### Mechanical pulp (SGW)

The simplest, and cheapest, method is either to tear the log apart using rotating steel discs armed with teeth, or to grind them down against a grindstone (the pulpstone) in hot water. The pulp produced using the latter method is known as stone-ground wood pulp. The yield from the original logs is very high, about 95–98 per cent, but the pulp contains all the ingredients that went into making that tree a tree. While some of these, like cellulose, are wanted, others like lignin (which binds the fibres together in the tree) and hemicelluloses are not. Paper made from this pulp is generally weak, and needs to be blended with about 20 per cent of wood-free pulp to give it the necessary strength. It discolours with age.

Mechanical pulp produces bulky papers with high opacity, and is used in newsprint and as base stock for lower grade printing papers.

### Refiner mechanical pulp (RMP)

The pulp produced using this process is slightly purer than mechanical pulp. In this process the smaller diameter wood, about 45 per cent of the tree, is broken down into small chips about 2cm square in a chipper, and then ground into pulp using disc refiners. Refiner mechanical pulp still contains lignin and hemi-celluloses, though less than mechanical pulp, which result in a paper that is weak and discolours with age.

### Thermomechanical pulp (TMP) and chemi-thermomechanical pulp (CTMP)

Pulps produced by these two processes become progressively purer, though they do not achieve the purity of chemical pulp. For TMP, the process again starts with chips, but this time they are treated with steam before they are ground into pulp. For CTMP the starting point is, again, chips, but this time, in addition to steam, they are treated with chemicals which dissolve out some, though not all, of the lignin and other impurities.

Papers made using CMTP are almost as good (and expensive) as papers produced from chemical pulp; but they will still discolour with age.

*Chemical pulp*

In the chemical pulping process the aim is to get rid of the lignin altogether. The chips are steam heated under pressure and impregnated with chemicals. The chips are then put into the digester, where they are cooked, again under high pressure and at high temperatures, and the lignin is dissolved. The fibres, now no longer held together by the lignin, are taken out of the digester to be washed and bleached; and the result is a lignin-free pure white pulp.

Paper produced from chemical pulp is strong, and does not discolour with age. It is sometimes (and confusingly) known as wood-free paper (or free sheet, in the USA). However, wood-free paper can contain up to 10 per cent mechanical pulp! If you want true wood-free paper, free of all traces of mechanical pulp, then you should ask for acid-free paper, which has a pH of 7. To add to the confusion, there is also a term – tree-free pulp – which refers to pulp made from recycled paper. To confuse matters completely, these two terms are used interchangeably, though they refer to entirely different products!

*Making the paper*

Paper making is done on sophisticated, high speed machines which convert pulp into paper. Production quantities obviously vary with the size of the paper mill, but a medium-sized mill is capable of producing 700–800 tonnes of paper a day.

A paper mill that uses the pulp it produces is known as an integrated mill.

Dried pulp is available in solid form, either in sheets or bales, and needs to be turned back into a liquid before it can be used.

This is done in a slusher or hydrapulper, which is like a giant mixing bowl, where the pulp is mixed with water and additives. These consist of:

- fillers or loadings, such as china clay, titanium dioxide, chalk and talc, which fill the spaces between the fibres and increase the paper's whiteness, smoothness and opacity
- pigments and dyes for colour and shade
- coatings, usually china clay and titanium dioxide, to give the paper a really smooth and flat surface
- sizing agents to reduce the paper's porosity and ability to absorb moisture, to prevent ink from feathering (or wicking) and to make the paper stronger and stiffer.

The liquid, known as stock (or stuff), now the colour and consistency of milk, passes through a refiner, which beats the fibres to open them out, separate them, and split their ends, so that they hook onto each other and form a continuous web (sheet) of paper during the paper making process.

The stock is screened twice to get rid of any impurities before being sucked up into the flow box (also known variously as the head box, or the stuff box) at the wet end of the paper making machine, from where it is released through a sluice onto a wire mesh.

This mesh (also known as the wire) is a fast-moving conveyor belt up to 10 metres wide, which, depending on the grade and weight of paper being made, can travel at speeds of up to 1000m a minute (60kph, or 40mph), as it carries the stock from the wet end to the dry end – a distance of some 35 metres. Acting like a giant sieve, the mesh allows the water to pass through it, while retaining the pulp fibres. By the time the fibres reach the drying rollers at the end of the wire they have formed into paper. As the wire travels along it shakes gently from side to side; the fibres pick up this shaking and align themselves to point in the direction of travel. This is known as machine direction, and is an important factor when you come to specifying paper for a job.

The paper passes through the drying rollers where its moisture content is reduced to 3–6 per cent. It is now ready to be cut into sheets, or smaller sized reels. But before this happens it can be subjected to a series of processes to enhance its properties – for example its smoothness by calendaring (or polishing) it; or its finish, by applying a coating of china clay; or to its absorbency by applying a sizing agent.

## Papers for books

The papers we are specifically interested in are those used by the publishing industry in books and publicity material, and they can be divided into two types: uncoated papers and coated papers.

These papers are known as book papers, and their properties have been specially formulated so that they can be easily printed and bound, and handled by the end user. Understanding these properties and the effect they have on the paper makes it easier to choose the right paper for the job.

Paper properties can be divided into two categories: physical and optical.

### *Physical properties*

#### *Weight, also known as substance, grammage and basis weight*

The weight of paper can be measured in grammes per square metre (gsm or $gm^2$), which is used almost everywhere in the world. However, if you are working in the USA or Canada, paper weight can be expressed in pounds per ream of 500 sheets.

Paper is sold by weight. So, generally speaking, the heavier the paper, the more it costs.

Book papers come in a fairly narrow range of weights, which starts at 60gsm and goes up to about 90gsm, in increments of 10gsm. Obviously, you can use lighter or heavier papers to suit the nature of the job.

For example, an 896-page paperback dictionary printed on a 90gsm paper weighs 1492g, but only 952g if printed on a 57gsm paper.

So, when choosing the paper weight, you need to think about:

- the cost of buying it
- the cost of transporting, handling and distributing the end product
- what it is like for the person using the end product.

Remember the following.

- Thick or bulky paper is not necessarily heavy. Paper bulk is determined by how much air there is between the fibres. For example look at how bulky and light a facial tissue is compared with the thickness and weight of the page you are reading.
- Light papers are not necessarily thin. For example, 100 sheets of a Vol.15 60gsm newsprint bulk 9mm, compared with 100 sheets of a Vol.9 90gsm offset paper, which bulk 8mm.
- Opacity does not necessarily increase with weight. For example, a 28gsm bible paper, which despite being lightweight has higher opacity than an 80gsm photocopier paper.

*Bulk, also known as caliper, thickness, gauge and volume basis*

This term describes the thickness of the paper, and specifies the ratio of its caliper to its substance. Printers are interested in bulk as it affects a paper's runnability (its behaviour on the press during printing and finishing) and printability (the printed quality of text and images). Publishers are interested in bulk, because it determines how thick the book is.

Paper bulk is expressed as its volume basis, written as Vol., followed by a number, which expresses the thickness in millimetres of 100 sheets of that paper in a substance of 100gsm. So, 100 sheets of a 100gsm Vol.20 paper will bulk 20mm/inches.

Low volume, or thin, papers have a low volume basis – for example, Vol.8; high volume, or thick, papers have a high volume basis – for example, Vol.20.

However, since not all books are 100 sheets (or 200 pages) long and printed on 100gsm paper, you need a formula to work out the bulk of your own book, and this appears below.

## How to calculate the bulk of your book

*Note: for the sake of simplicity, all answers have been rounded up.*

The formula for calculating bulk where the volume basis is known is:

gsm × volume × half the extent/10,000 = bulk in millimetres

What is the bulk of a 688 page book, printed on a 90gsm paper, with a volume basis of 15?

90gsm × Vol.15 × 344 sheets/10,000 = 46mm

What will the bulk of the same book be if printed on a 90gsm paper with a volume basis of 20?
  Answer: 90gsm × Vol.20 × 344 sheets/10,000 = 62mm

And what will it be if printed on a 90gsm Vol.11 paper?
  Answer: 90gsm × Vol.11 × 344 sheets/10,000 = 34mm

It is also possible to work out the volume basis you need in order to achieve a desired bulk. For example, if you want to achieve a bulk of 52mm for the above book, printed on a 90gsm paper, what volume basis do you need to specify?

90gsm × 344 sheets/10,000 = 3.096
52mm/3.096 = 17
Answer: a Vol.17 paper is needed.

Using the formulae in the example above allows you to work out the bulk of the book, and avoids the need for a dummy to be made. Knowing the book (or spine) bulk is essential for jacket design and for binding.

Be aware that bulky paper may cause difficulties in folding, as there is a limit to how many times it is possible to fold a bulky sheet. If you are thinking of using a bulky paper, check with the binder first.

It would certainly cost more if you suddenly found that you had to fold and sew 8 × 16-page sections, because the paper was too bulky to be folded as 4 × 32-page sections.

Knowing the weight and bulk of a paper, means that you can work out things like:

- how many books you can fit into a binder's parcel – limited on grounds of health and safety to a maximum of 13.5kg
- how many books you can fit onto a pallet – limited by weight and height
- how many books can fit into a lorry load
- how many books you can fit into a container

and all the associated costs of packing and transportation.

*Grain*

This term is used to describe the direction in which the fibres lie as they are being formed into paper. Where they lie parallel with the direction of travel, the grain is known as machine direction, or long grain. Where the grain is at right angles to the direction of travel it is known as cross-direction or short grain.

Grain is important when it comes to sheeting, and paper destined for book work should ideally be long grain, as it folds more easily. Books bound with the grain running parallel with the spine lie (and stay) flat when opened.

There are two rough and ready tests for telling grain direction. One is to take a sheet of paper and tear it lengthwise (without folding it). Long-grain paper tears quite easily and roughly in a straight line. Short-grain paper is less easy to tear and does so in a random series of zigzags.

The other test is to cut a piece of paper about $25 \times 50mm$ (one inch by two), and wet it. As the paper dries it will curl into a tube. The direction of the curl shows that the paper is short- (or cross-) grained.

Knowing about grain direction is only helpful if you are able to do something about it, and this is not always practicable. For example, if you start out with a long-grain sheet, and fold it once, the result is a sheet where the grain runs across, and not parallel, with the spine fold. Fold it again, and the grain is now parallel once more. The art to this is that you need to work out the final page size of your book in relation to the size of the sheet you are folding (though not necessarily printing), and to see if the final fold enables you to finish up with the grain going in the right direction – up and down the spine. (see Figure 5.1 on p. 112)

This is relatively simple when your books are being produced on a sheet-fed press, and sheets are folded after being printed.

The grain direction in the reels of paper used for web printing is always long grain – that is, it runs with the length of the paper around the reel, and not across it. When your book is being produced on a web press, where the final output is a folded section, the dimensions of the press – its width and the diameter of its impression cylinder/blanket (cut-off) may make it impossible to come up with long-grain sections.

Grain direction is important because it does have an effect on your end product. So, it is certainly worth discussing your binding requirements and specification with the printer and/or binder before you start ordering paper.

In the end, though, you should bear in mind that while it is nice to have books where the grain runs parallel with the spine, there are also plenty of books in the shops where this is not the case, particularly when it comes to mass market paperbacks. In the end it most often comes down to a question of cost, fitness for purpose, and having to do the best with what is available in terms of money, raw materials and equipment.

### Smoothness (also known as finish)

This term is used to describe the surface of the paper, and its contour, and is important for the printer.

Paper in its natural state has a slightly rough texture, which can be made smooth by calendaring. Calendars are stainless steel rollers, situated online at the dry end of the paper-making machine, which polish the paper as it passes between them.

Light calendaring produces a machine finished, or MF, paper which is frequently used in offset printing, mainly for monochrome line or halftone work.

Further calendaring, known as supercalendaring, can be done offline, to produce a smoother, shiny paper. However, supercalendaring does reduce the paper's opacity to the point that you have the beginnings of greaseproof paper, which you can use as tracing paper – if you are really need some and have not got the real stuff to hand.

Smoothness can also be achieved by the use of china clay as a filler in the pulp, which produces a paper known as imitation art.

True art paper is made by adding a china clay coating to the paper once it has been made.

Art papers come with finishes from matt, through silk/satin (or semi-matt), to glossy.

Most paper produced today is wove, whose chief characteristics are its surface uniformity and the lack of any visible texture. For example, photocopying paper is wove, as is paper used in newspapers, and most books. By contrast, laid paper has a ribbed texture which comes from the lay lines of the mould in which paper was traditionally made before the advent of paper-making machinery like the Fourdrinier machine. Laid papers are still made, and used, though in small quantities, particularly for stationery and fine printing.

*Formation*

Describes the way the fibres and fillers are distributed in the finished sheet. Even distribution throughout the sheet is an important property, as it has an effect on the other properties of the sheet such as opacity, strength and printability. Formation can be checked by holding the sheet up to light. In evenly formed paper the fibres and fillers are distributed uniformly across the sheet to produce a consistent look. Unevenly formed paper, known as wild paper, is pretty much that – with fibres and fillers forming dark clusters across the sheet, giving the impression of a wild moonlit sky.

*Moisture*

All paper contains moisture, expressed as a percentage of its weight, and moisture content varies according to atmospheric conditions like temperature and relative humidity. For book papers used in offset lithographic printing optimum moisture content is five to six per cent. Moisture content is important as it is has a direct effect on how easily it runs through the printing and finishing processes (its runnability), and on how well it accepts text and images (its printability). Paper where the moisture content is just slightly higher than the norm tends to produce the best results.

If paper is too dry, it will absorb moisture from the air. However, this cannot occur uniformly, as moisture is absorbed across (or against), the grain rather than with the grain (or along it). This causes problems with dimensional

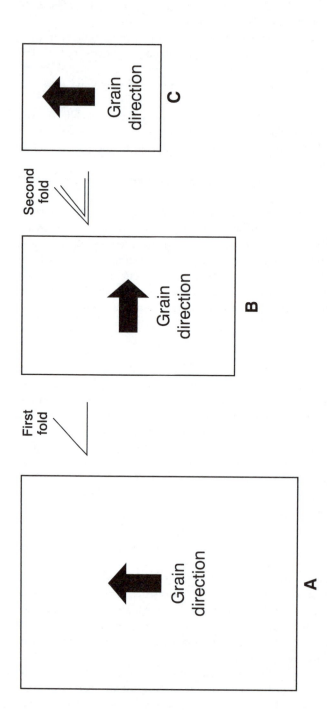

## How folding affects grain direction

A: an unfolded long grain sheet

B: the same sheet folded once: a portrait book using this sheet would be wrong grain, which should be avoided if possible

C: the same sheet folded once more: a portrait book bound using this sheet would be long grain, which is acceptable

*Figure 5.1* The effects of folding on grain direction

stability, which is critical for accurate register in 4-colour printing. It also results in cockling (see below).

So, if paper has just arrived at the printer's, it is important to give it time to adjust itself (known as conditioning) to the humidity of its new environment before it is put on press – generally about two days.

Moisture content is less important in web printing than in sheet-fed printing.

### Optical properties

#### Whiteness, brightness and shade

These three terms describe the appearance of paper to the eye. They are three distinct properties, but are often used interchangeably, which is a mistake:

- *whiteness* is a measure of the reflectance of all the wavelengths of light across the whole spectrum
- *brightness* is a measure of the reflectance of the wavelength of blue light, so it involves only a fraction of the spectrum
- *shade* is a measure of the paper's colour.

Shade is divided into three groups:

- true white – which reflects the complete spectrum, and is often described as neutral
- cream white – which absorbs the cool, blue end of the spectrum and reflects the warm yellow end. Cream-white papers have a creamy cast
- blue white – which absorbs the warm colours, and reflects blue.

Blue-white papers are known as high- or bright white, and are popular with publishers and readers because they appear brighter and whiter than true- or cream-white papers.

In book publishing, shade is an important factor in paper choice, and should reflect the needs of the job, as well as those of the reader. It is also important to consider content, purpose and fitness for purpose.

For example, when choosing paper for a novel, which might involve sustained reading for long periods of time, it is advisable to choose either a true- or a cream-white paper for the job. There is less contrast between the black of the text and the background on which it appears, and this makes it visually comfortable for the reader.

High-white papers are ideal for colour work, where their whiteness and bright-ness give a lift to the illustrations, especially if the colours are predominantly from the cool end of the spectrum.

Colour work on true-white or cream-white papers can work, but the way they reflect light does have an effect on the way colours appear on the page by warming them up and deadening them at the same time, which is undesirable in something like a medical book, where printed illustrations need to match the original subject as closely as possible, if they are to serve their intended purpose.

Brightness can be boosted by the use of optical brightening agents (OBA).

## Opacity

A paper's opacity is the degree to which it prevents light from passing through it (show through). Paper, such as a coated art, which allows no light to pass through it, is 100 per cent opaque. The opacity of a 60gsm tracing paper is about 25 per cent; while for uncoated paper, like newsprint, it is about 90–94 per cent.

Opacity needs to be considered when both sides of the paper are to be printed on, since it is undesirable for the material appearing on one side of the sheet to be seen from the other, and interfere with legibility and readability.

So, for example, a heavily illustrated school book where text and illustrations appear randomly on both sides of the sheet, opacity is a critical issue, and you may well have to choose a paper with 100 per cent opacity. However, in a newspaper, which still carries a lot of randomly placed pictures and text, opacity is less of an issue, and 90–94 per cent opacity is acceptable.

This is also true for work where there are few, if any, illustrations, and where lines of text are printed back to back (back each other up) on each side of the paper, and have the effect of cancelling each other out.

The way to check a paper's opacity is to put a plain unprinted sheet over something that has been printed, and to see how easy it is to see the printing. If you can see it through the superimposed sheet, it means that opacity is low. You should also ask for printed samples, and make your judgement on these.

As mentioned earlier, opacity is a combination of several factors including density, formation and coating, but not weight. A particular paper in 90gsm with low opacity will not become more opaque by increasing its weight. All that happens is that the paper costs more, and the book gets heavier! In this case you should be looking for a different paper.

### Miscellaneous properties of paper

Paper has a wide range of physical properties in addition to the ones discussed above. Most of these are of more interest and importance to the printer and binder, as these properties affect how a certain paper behaves while it is being printed and bound, and on how well it reproduces text and images.

These include:

- compressibility – its ability to change its surface contour when in contact with printing surfaces
- folding strength – its tolerance to multiple folding – especially important in books and maps
- stretch – its ability to withstand distortion when being printed – especially important in web printing

- tearing resistance – an important consideration in web printing
- tensile strength – an indication of the length and strength of the fibres in the paper, and how well they have bonded during paper making.

## Choosing paper

By now we should have a pretty good idea of how paper is made, and of the properties that make it more or less suitable for particular kinds of work.

### Choosing the right paper for the job

The first thing that strikes you when you first start looking at what is available is the enormous range to choose from – newsprint, wood-free, laid, wove, cartridge, MF, SC, imitation art, art – to mention just a few. The second is: 'Where on Earth do I start?'

The simple answer is to start by defining the end product in terms of its:

- format
- extent
- use of colour
- binding style.

Having done this, you need to define what you are trying to end up with in terms of:

- production costs, selling price and value for money
- production values and overall quality, in terms of look, feel and durability
- fitness for purpose
- printability
- runnability.

Doing this makes choosing a lot easier.

## Case studies

Rather than dealing in abstracts, it's easier to work with a series of case studies, which start with monochrome work, progress to combined monochrome and colour work, and end with integrated colour.

### Case study 5.1: monochrome

This involves a 768-page mass market paperback, with a print run of 150,000 copies, perfect bound. Sales and marketing want the book to bulk round about 40–45mm, and are aiming for a recommended retail price of £7.99.

So, production costs, particularly paper, need to be tightly controlled in order to make the £7.99 recommended retail price possible.

For a book like this, I would choose a Vol.8, 70gsm mechanical or semi-mechanical paper – probably a bulky newsprint – in reels, so that it can be printed on a web offset press.

We already know that this kind of paper is weak, and discolours with age. Its shade is often off-white, with a marked tendency towards greyness, and it is also quite absorbent. But these are acceptable trade-offs in return for its relative cheapness (up to 35 per cent less than a 70gsm MF offset which is stronger and does not discolour with age).

It bulks nicely, and folds and binds well. It is reasonably light: 649g for 768 pages, plus cover, as against 829g, if it had been printed on a 90gsm MF paper; and it has good opacity, though this is not an important consideration, since the book is text only with lines that back each other up.

If this paper works well for newspapers, and it does, there is every reason to believe that it will work well for this book.

Ideally, I would like a long-grain paper which runs parallel with the spine when the book is bound. However, as mentioned earlier, if the book is being printed on a web press, this may be difficult to manage, and is, therefore, something to discuss with the printer and binder, before you make your decision.

In light of all these factors, I would choose this type and weight of paper; and then present it, with reasons for my choice, to the editor and sales and marketing, just to make sure they like it, too.

## Case study 5.2: monochrome

An 80-page poetry book, size 216 × 138mm, section sewn in paperback. The run is about 250 copies, which is quite good for this genre, and it has been decided to print it sheet-fed offset, though the small run would make it a strong candidate for digital printing. The market is small, and is avidly dedicated to the work of this poet. So, as far as sales and marketing are concerned, the price of £14.99 is less of a consideration for the purchaser than being able to buy the book, and the fact that it is nicely printed and bound, and the paper is good quality.

When choosing the paper for this book, I need to think of these things.

- Bulk: 80 pages are not going to bulk very much unless we go for a quite high volume paper, say, Vol.28. This gives me a bulk of 10mm, which is acceptable. Books with thin spines don't stand out on a bookshelf in a bookshop very well at the best of times, and even less so if the spine is so thin that you either can't fit any type on it, or the type has to be so small to fit that it is virtually invisible.

- Weight and finish: 90gsm MF offset book wove, which gives the book a good feel in terms of weight and ease of handling. The machine finish produces a smoother paper than newsprint, but leaves just enough residual roughness (known as 'tooth') for it to be interesting. This can be felt by rubbing the sheet between your forefinger and thumb – a good habit to adopt when you are working with paper, especially when it is new to you. If I really want to increase the visual production values, I might think of using a laid paper to give the book a visual cachet. However, since this might not be to everyone's taste (perhaps not even the poet's), it is important to check with the editor and sales and marketing first. Laid paper must finish up long grain, so that the lay lines run up and down the page and not across it. Lay lines running across the page look unsightly, and are likely to interfere with the reader's visual comfort and the readability of the page. Again, something that needs to be checked with the printer and binder before making the decision. Personally, I quite like a laid paper for stationery, but think it looks odd in a book.
- Shade: true- or cream white in preference to a blue white, to reduce the contrast between the paper and the blackness of the type, and make it visually comfortable for the reader.
- Opacity: poetry setting, unlike novel setting, is generally rather random: there are short lines, long lines, short poems and long poems. This means that opacity is important.
- Pulp type: a wood-free paper, but happy to make do with a paper that might contain a small percentage of mechanical pulp.
- Grain: ideally, a long grain; but would not matter if it were short grain.

## Case study 5.3: monochrome and colour – not integrated

This case study concerns a 384-page, 234 × 156mm, section sewn hardback biography, with 4 × 8-page sections of illustrations, with a print run of 3,500 copies. The run length means that it is to be printed sheet-fed offset. The text is to be printed in black ink only on an uncoated offset paper, while the illustrations are to be printed in 4-colour on a matt coated art paper. The book will retail at a recommended retail price of £25; and production values are fairly high. It is possible to print the entire book on coated paper, and have the pictures scattered throughout the book, as if it were integrated. However, with so few pictures, it has been decided to group them together in sections printed on a good quality art paper. Doing this has several advantages.

- Paper costs: the cost of paper would increase by 12 per cent if the whole book were printed on art paper.
- Book weight: the book weight would increase by 18 per cent to 862g, which is not comfortable for the reader to hold for long periods of time.
- Printing costs: if the book were printed 4-colour throughout, the printing costs would increase by 68 per cent. For a book of this kind, it clearly makes more sense to print it as two separate components, and bring them together during binding. However, mainly for marketing reasons, not all books can be printed with separate illustration sections.

Text

- Bulk: I would choose a Vol.26 paper, which would give me a bulk of 45mm between boards. If the extent is longer, I have the choice of sticking with the Vol.26 paper and ending up with a thicker book; or of reducing the volume to maintain bulk at around 45mm.
- Weight: 90gsm.
- Finish: wove.
- Shade: true white or cream white; though, probably true white to match more closely the paper used for the illustrations.
- Opacity: although text lines back each other up, opacity is important in this book, so I would check this.
- Pulp type: wood free, with some mechanical content.
- Grain: long.

Illustrations

- Bulk: not really relevant for such a small number of pages.
- Weight: 100gsm.
- Finish: matt coated art paper. I have chosen a matt art (paper) because it has a dull finish that does not reflect or glare under artificial light, which happens with glossy art. I could have chosen a semi matt or silk finish (slightly glossy) paper, and achieved much the same effect, but my personal preference is for matt art.
- Shade: blue white.
- Opacity: with art paper opacity should be 100 per cent.

- Pulp type: wood free, with some mechanical content. The coating mitigates to quite a large extent the properties associated with mechanical pulp: adding strength to the sheet, brightness and whiteness to the shade, and eliminating discolouration.
- Grain: long.

## Case study 5.4: monochrome and colour/integrated

This is a 352-page, hardback cookery book, art book – products where production values need to be reasonably high. Text and illustrations appear on the same page (integrated), and bleed. There is a lot of solid ink on each page, with type reversed out.

- Bulk: I would choose a Vol.14 paper, which would give me a bulk of 25mm between boards.
- Weight: 100gsm.
- Finish: matt coated art paper.
- Shade: blue white, to give the pictures lift, and make them bright and attractive.
- Opacity: 100 per cent.
- Pulp type: wood free, with a small amount of mechanical pulp.
- Grain: long.

## Case study 5.5: long extent: monochrome and colour/integrated

Finally, we come to books with very long extents, either monochrome or colour, for example: a 1472-page dictionary, a 1952-page encyclopaedia, the collected works of Shakespeare, where bulk and weight are critical, in order to stop the book becoming either too heavy or too bulky.

The paper best suited to this kind of work is a coated paper, called a lightweight thin opaque, which basically says all there is to say about it. It is:

- lightweight – starting around 27 and going up to 57gsm.
- thin – low volume starting at Vol.8.
- opaque – high opacity, in spite of its thinness.

This kind of paper is also known as India paper or bible paper, and is generally made from chemical pulp, so that it is often neutral with a pH of 7.

A 234 × 156mm, 1472-page paperback dictionary printed on a 35gsm Vol.10 lightweight thin opaque paper will weigh 960g (which includes 20g for the cover), and bulk 26mm. Just as a matter of interest, if you had chosen the same paper for this job as used for the poetry book, it would weigh 2.4kg, and bulk 164mm! Unlikely, but it certainly does point up what a critical role bulk and weight play when choosing a paper.

This paper takes colour very well, because of its coating, which makes it very white (true or blue white) and very smooth.

The only drawback to using lightweight paper in grammages below 50gsm comes from problems with runnability – on sheet-fed presses (and during folding). It is because they are so lightweight, that machine speed needs to be drastically reduced: typically down to 1200–1500 impressions (or sheets) per hour against the more usual speeds of 10,000–15,000. This means that a job that would normally take one hour to print can now take ten. So, if you do intend to use lightweight paper, make sure the printer and binder know this when you are planning the job and asking for estimates.

The best way to print lightweight papers is on a web press, which delivers a neatly folded section, and eliminates any problems caused by low grammage.

So far, we have been looking at how to choose paper for the text. We now need to think about paper for the endpapers, for the jacket, for the cover and for the printed paper case (PPC), case wrap or cover-to-board.

## Endpapers

Endpapers (usually known as ends) need to be strong and sturdy, as part of their job is to hold the case and the book block together. Endpaper grammage can start as low as 120gsm, and work upwards to about 150gsm. A common preference is for a 135gsm cartridge.

Grain should always be long wherever possible. Short-grain endpapers will cockle or crease, especially when they come in contact with the paste used to attach them to the case.

Ends can be plain white, in which case their shade should match as closely as possible the shade of the paper in the book block. They can be coated, or uncoated, which, again, depends on the shade of the paper in the book block.

They can also be dyed (or self-coloured), and you choose the colour from a sample book, supplied by the printer/binder.

Ends can also be printed using a PMS colour on one or both sides of the sheet. Since there is no detail, paper for ends printed this way can be uncoated or coated, depending on cost, as well as taste. If printing on one side only of a coated paper, it is worth asking for a single-sided art paper (where the coating is on one side only of the sheet) – the coated side being used to print on, the uncoated side being left plain and facing the first page of the book block.

Finally, ends can be printed 4-colour. When this happens, use a good quality single- or double-sided art paper. To reproduce the pictures at their best, it is best to choose a blue-white shade.

## (Dust) jacket

The dust jacket is the loose outer wrapping round a hardback book, and is made of paper. There are several types of papers to choose from, depending very much on the effect you are trying to create.

Most jackets are designed to catch the eye of the reader-in-waiting, which generally involves bright 4-colour printing, lamination, and spot UV varnish. The best paper for this sort of work is a single-sided art paper, starting at 125gsm (which I use as standard), and going up to about 150gsm. It has a blue-white shade, and should be long grain. Single-sided art is cheaper than double-sided, and is more practical since the roughness of the uncoated inner side of the jacket creates friction between jacket and book, and prevents it from slipping or sliding off.

However, if you are trying to recreate a retro-looking jacket, the paper to choose would be a heavy (130gsm) rough cartridge paper, printed using a PMS colour. However, because of its roughness, this paper does not take 4-colour printing particularly well, and it is also difficult to laminate. But since single colour printing and unlaminated jackets were, and are, the hallmarks of old-fashioned production values, the problem does not really arise.

## Printed paper case, or case wrap, or cover to board

Paper can be used as an alternative to cloth to cover the case of a hardback book. The paper most commonly used for this is a 125gsm single-sided, long-grain, blue-white art, which must be able to take the glue used to stick it to the case.

### Cover

A paperback book is protected by its cover, which is made of board (the term conventionally given to any paper with a substance that exceeds 200gsm), though it is often called cover card.

The cover needs to be strong to withstand day-to-day wear and tear, and most cover card for books starts at 220gsm working its way in 20gsm units up to about 280gsm – with an average weight being 240gsm.

Covers, like jackets, are generally printed in 4-colour, so the card needs to be bright and white (blue white), and the grain needs to be long grain to prevent problems with binding and bound copies. Since the card is being printed on one side only, it makes sense to use a single-sided card.

We have now reached the point where we can be fairly competent at, and confident in, choosing a paper for a job being printed by offset lithography – either sheet-fed or web.

### Case board

The case used for hardback, or cased, books is made from cloth and board (front board and back board) glued together. Where there once existed a host of names each one denoting a specific type of board for a specific type of job, there is now one common name – binder's board, which makes things a lot easier, if more prosaic.

If the robustness of the case and its ability to withstand normal wear and tear, and not get bent or dented corners are important, then you should discuss various options – such as millboard – with the binder.

Binder's boards come in various weights expressed in gsm or old-fashioned ounces (ozs) which are still used, and thicknesses expressed in microns or thousandths of an inch.

*Table 5.1* Binder's board weights

| Microns | 1000ths" | gsm | Ounces | Book sizes |
|---------|----------|-----|--------|------------|
| 1700 | 0.070 | 1100 | 24 | Crown 8vo, Large crown 8vo |
| 2000 | 0.080 | 1300 | 28 | Demy 8vo, Royal 8vo |
| 2300 | 0.090 | 1500 | 32 | Crown 4to, Demy 4to |
| 2900 | 0.115 | 1900 | 40 | Demy 4to, A4 |

When choosing a board weight, it is important to match the weight and thickness to the book's size: the bigger the book the heavier and thicker the boards.

## Choosing paper for digital printing

An increasingly common technology is digital printing, used for print on demand (POD) and short-run work. While its main use is for monochrome work, it is now starting to be used successfully for colour work as well.

POD, by its nature, involves producing mostly single copies as part of a continuous workflow on a web press: as soon as one book is printed, work starts on the next; so that, typically, 20 different titles may be produced in an hour of printing, which makes it virtually impossible for anyone other than the printer to supply the paper.

Although short-run printing quantities are higher than POD, it is still easier and more efficient in terms of time, cost and quality, for the printer to supply the paper.

So, the general rule is that digital printers supply their own paper.

For laser printed monochrome POD work paper is generally an 80–90gsm white MF offset paper, which is reasonably opaque and runs well on the press.

For laser printed colour POD work paper is generally a 100–110gsm matt coated art paper. Opacity is excellent, and it runs well on press.

A recent development, and one that is likely to have an impact on the digital market, is inkjet printing.

Where laser printing uses extremes of temperature to fuse text and images to the page using dry, or liquid, toner, inkjet printing uses water-based inks which are squirted onto the paper through a series of nozzles to create text and images.

Paper for laser printing needs to withstand extremes of temperature, and moisture content has to be carefully controlled during manufacture to ensure smooth running on the press, and to prevent problems like misfeeding, jamming or tearing.

With inkjet printing, the main problem arises with uncoated papers where ink may travel along the fibres (wicking) to cause feathering. This can be prevented by using a properly sized paper, or changing to a coated paper.

Paper manufacturers are doing a lot to produce paper specifically formulated to run on digital presses, which is increasingly necessary as digital printing rapidly becomes the preferred method of producing printed pages.

## Paper defects in printing: runnability and printability

Paper is a complex mixture of fibres, fillers, coating and other ingredients, which give it a wide range of properties that vary from making to making. While the paper mill does everything it can to maintain a consistently high standard, defects do occur, which affect the paper's runnability and printability, as much as the quality of the finished product.

There is some ambiguity about exactly where runnability becomes printability, as both terms overlap.

Nevertheless, a useful definition of runnability is: the ease with which paper moves through the printing press.

Runnable paper is:

- uniform in formation
- strong and tear resistant
- dimensionally stable
- properly conditioned, and has been given time to adapt to the temperature and humidity of where it is to be printed
- precision cut
- suitably stiff for ease of handling
- water resistant.

For printability a useful definition is: a paper's suitability for a given printing process, and how well it works with ink when it is being printed.

Printable paper must:

- be uniformly formed, without variation or irregularity
- be able to accept ink, and allow it to dry quickly
- have a strong surface to prevent picking during printing
- have low absorbency and good ink hold out
- be smooth
- have good opacity.

Most of the defects listed below occur during printing, and should be dealt with by the printer. Sometimes, though, they can carry through to the finished product, in which case it ends up with the publisher having to identify and deal with them.

### Build-up (also known as piling)

The accumulation of chemicals, ink and paper dust or particles on the printing plate, or blanket, which causes hickeys as well as loss of definition in halftone work.

### Contraries

Foreign bodies and dirt in the paper.

### Fish eye

A white, translucent spot most generally found in coated papers, and caused by fibre bundles or incorrectly prepared chemicals.

### Hickeys

White spots in areas of solid colour, caused by build-up of paper dust or particles on the printing plate or blanket.

### Linting

The build-up of loose fibres from the paper's surface fibres (also known as lint or fluff). Lint can cause fibre build-up in the printed image areas, especially when the lint mixes with ink. A common cause of hickeys.

### Picking

Ink-coated paper fibres pull out of the paper surface during printing. These fibres build up during printing and cause hickeys.

### Piping

Moisture wrinkles, or creases, running in the machine direction of a reel (or web) of paper, caused by non-uniform absorption of moisture and causing expansion across the grain.

*Shade variation*

Shade can vary between one batch of paper and another of the same paper. So, it is important to make sure that batches are not mixed during printing, resulting in a product with multiple shades in it.

## Paper defects in binding

Most of the problems that occur with paper do so at the printing stage. Nevertheless, there are some problems that will occur only during binding. Luckily, they are few in number:

*Cockling*

Pages in a bound book develop waves, caused by non-uniform drying and shrinkage in paper that has not been allowed to condition adequately, or where the book has been laser printed using heat, and the paper has lost a lot of its moisture in the process. The problem may disappear with time, especially if the book is stored flat. However, it can recur in damp conditions.

*Cracking*

Separation of the coating from the substrate along the fold. Occurs in coated papers that have been over-dried.

## Calculating paper quantities – sheet-fed work

Calculating the amount of paper needed for a job is relatively simple, provided two basic facts are kept in mind:

- a sheet of paper has two sides, each side counts as one page
- sheet sizes are related to book sizes: so, demy sheets are for demy books, crown sheets are for crown books, and so on.

Armed with this information it is possible to avoid ordering twice or half the amount of paper needed for a job.

*Calculating the number of sheets needed for a job*

You need to know the:

- extent of the book
- number of copies to be printed
- number of pages that can be fitted onto each side of a sheet of paper.

The first two are straightforward.
　　The third depends on the dimensions of the book and the size of the sheet.

The easiest way to find out is to ask the printer these questions.

- How many pages will there be in a section (or signature, the terms can be used interchangeably)? (This is the most direct way of asking, and the answer is unambiguous – for example, 32 pages.)
- How many pages will be printed to view? (In this question, the printer is being asked how many pages will be printed on each side of the sheet. On the basis that it is only possible to view one side of the sheet at a time, the answer should be doubled to get the right number of pages. So, if the answer is 16 pages to view, then the section is a 32-page section.)

If you are unable to ask the printer, there is a formula for calculating sheet quantities:

$$\frac{extent \times print\ run}{pages\ per\ section}$$

Example:

How many sheets of paper are needed to print 3,000 copies of a 192 page book, printed 16 pages to view?

If each side of the paper is printed 16 pages to view, each section will consist of 32 pages (2 sides of 16 pages each)

$$\frac{192pp \times 3,000}{32\ pages\ per\ section}$$

The answer is 18,000 sheets, to which should be added an amount for spoilage (see below).

If you are having a problem finding out how many pages are to be printed to view, take the dimensions of the trimmed page size, and add:

6mm to the height, and 3mm to the width

This gives you the untrimmed page size.

Example:

The trimmed page size of a Royal 8vo book is 234 × 156mm, and its un-trimmed size is 240 × 159mm.

Take the quad sheet size (960 × 1272mm) for a Royal 8vo book: divide the untrimmed page width into the sheet width, and the page height into the sheet length:

$$\frac{960mm = 4\ and\ 1272mm\ =\ 8}{240mm\ \times\ 159mm}$$

4 × 8 pages = 32 pages on one side of the sheet

## Standard book and sheet sizes

Most books are produced in standard metric book publishing formats. These are given below for non-bleeding, portrait work:

*Table 5.2* Format sizes

| Format | Trimmed page size in mm |
|---|---|
| Crown 8vo | 186 × 123 |
| Crown 4to | 246 × 189 |
| Large crown 8vo | 198 × 129 |
| Demy 8vo | 216 × 138 |
| Demy 4to | 276 × 219 |
| Royal 8vo | 234 × 156 |
| Royal 4to | 312 × 237 |

Below are the sheet sizes for each format designed to fit the press on which the job is to be printed. Sizes are given in their actual form, as well as their rounded form which is how they are sold:

*Table 5.3* Format sheet sizes

| Format | Actual quad sheet size in mm | Rounded quad sheet size in mm |
|---|---|---|
| Crown 8vo | 768(M) × 1008 | 770(M) × 1010 |
| Crown 4to | 768 × 1008(M) | 770 × 1010(M) |
| Large crown 8vo | 816(M) × 1056 | 820(M) × 1060 |
| Demy 8vo | 888(M) × 1128 | 890(M) × 1130 |
| Demy 4to | 888 × 1128(M) | 890 × 1130(M) |
| Royal 8vo | 960(M) × 1272 | 960(M) × 1270 |
| Royal 4to | 960 × 1272(M) | 960 × 1270(M) |

The (M) immediately following the dimension in the 4to formats indicates that the sheets are long grain, and that the book will be bound long grain – that is, with the grain running parallel with the spine. Similarly, all the 8vo books will be bound cross- or short-grain, with the grain running from side to side across the book.

It is useful to know that:

- octavo (8vo) books printed on quad (4) sheets carry 32 pages to view, and produce 64 page sections
- quarto (4to) books printed on quad (4) sheets carry 16 pages to view, and produce 32 page sections

- octavo (8vo) books, printed on double quad (8) sheets carry 64-pages to view, or 128-page sections
- quarto (4to) books printed on double quad sheets carry 32 pages to view, and produce 64-page sections.

## Calculating paper quantities – web-fed work

Again, you need to know the extent and the print run, as well as the number of pages carried on each side of the paper.

However, because paper for web presses comes on reels, and not in sheets, you have to work out the sheet size based on the reel width, and the size of the press cut-off, which is what cuts the printed reel into lengths.

With this information, you can work out the number of pages printed to view in exactly the same way as you would for a sheet.

As an example, a 234 × 156mm book, printed on an 960mm wide reel on a press with a 640mm cut-off, produces a sheet with 16 pages to view, or a 32-page section.

This means that every 32 page section of this book uses 640mm (or .64 of a metre) of paper on a reel.

Imagine the same book, but with an extent of 320 pages. If each section uses .64m of paper, then 10 × 32-page sections will use 6.4m of paper; and to print 3,500 copies of the book uses 6.4m × 3,500 copies = 22,400 metres, plus spoilage.

Below are the common reel widths for the range of standard book formats:

*Table 5.4* Common reel widths

| Book format | Reel width |
| --- | --- |
| Crown 8vo/4to | 770mm |
| Large crown 8vo | 820mm |
| Demy 8vo/4to | 890mm |
| Royal 8vo/4to | 960mm |

For mass market A format and B format paperbacks, typical reel widths are shown below, most of which will produce cross-grained books.

*Table 5.5* Mass market reel widths

| Trimmed page size | Format | Reel width | Pages per section |
| --- | --- | --- | --- |
| 178 × 111mm | A | 1104mm | 96 |
| 178 × 111mm | A | 1472mm | 128 |
| 198 × 129mm | B | 1224mm | 96 |

### Non-standard book sizes

Most books tend to be produced in the standard formats. This is because it is economical to do so: standard sized papers are readily available, and fit onto standard sized presses and binding lines. These formats have evolved over time, they are liked by end users, and fit neatly onto retailers' shelves. Nevertheless, there are inevitably those occasions when a standard format is not appropriate, and a non-standard format is called for – for example, an exhibition catalogue or a manual.

If the first print run is a really long one, and the extent is long, it should be possible to have paper specially made for the job.

This may be alright for the first impression, but what happens if you have to do a reprint which may not be large enough to make it economical for the paper mill, producing 30–35 tonnes of paper an hour, to produce a special making for you?

For example, a print run of 100,000 copies of a 512-page 225 × 225mm book, printed on a 100gsm paper, would need about 139 tonnes of paper (including spoilage), or about 4 hours' worth of production. So, making the paper for a 15,000 copy reprint would take only 35 minutes or so, which is clearly not a viable proposition for the paper mill.

If the first print run (or reprint) is too short to warrant a mill making, you will have to print on an oversize standard sheet, and trim off the extra paper (cutting to waste) to arrive at the desired format.

In the example above, 31 per cent of the paper would be cut to waste if that book is printed on a standard sheet; which would certainly make it worth thinking seriously about the implications of producing a non-standard format book.

### Working out a sheet size for a non-standard format book

To do this, add 6mm to the height and 3mm to the width of the trimmed page size, to give you the untrimmed page size.

Then multiply the height and the width by 4, to obtain the sheet size for a 32-page section – that is, printed 16 pages to view.

Example:

Take a book with a trimmed page size of 225 × 225mm, and add 6mm to the height and 3mm to the width = untrimmed page size of 231 × 228mm.

Multiply the height and the width by 4 = a sheet size of 924 × 912mm, rounded = 930 × 920mm.

### Spoilage (wastage)

Spoilage or wastage is the term used for the paper lost or wasted through problems during printing and binding, and through the need for make ready.

To be able to deliver the required quantity of finished books, the printer and binder need extra paper, known as the spoilage allowance. The exact amount of the allowance must be agreed between the supplier and the customer, since it is the customer who pays for the extra paper.

Example:

For a job requiring a basic 1,000 sheets, with a five per cent spoilage allowance, the customer will have to pay for 1050 sheets.

On a historical note, it is interesting to note that a ream is either 500 or 516 sheets of paper. A 516-sheet ream is a printer's ream, and includes a 3.2 per cent spoilage allowance for printing and binding; a 500-sheet ream is a stationer's ream. There is also a 480-sheet ream, known as a short ream.

The spoilage allowance varies from job to job according to:

- type of printing – sheet- or web-fed
- length of print run
- number of colours
- the type of binding
- paper weight and finish
- additional processes – for example, lamination, varnishing.

Typical spoilage allowances for monochrome sheet-fed work start at 6.5 per cent (4 per cent for the printer and 2.5 per cent for the binder) for runs between 1,000 and 2,500 copies, gradually dropping to 3.5 per cent (2.5 per cent + 1 per cent) for 10,000 copies upwards. For colour work 2 per cent is added to the printer's allowance.

For monochrome web work, the allowances are higher, starting at 11 per cent + 1 per cent for 10,000–15,000 copies, and dropping to 5 per cent + 1 per cent for 75,000 copies and up. For colour work, add 3 per cent to the printer's allowance.

Although the spoilage allowance is there to ensure that the quantity ordered is the quantity delivered, printers and publishers are aware that paper is expensive, not only in terms of what it costs to make, but also in terms of its cost to the environment. With this in mind, printers, generally, strive to reduce their wastage to below the BPIF guidelines. (Further discussion on this topic and greenness in general appears later in this chapter.)

## Paper and the environment

Paper is an organic product, and its production in terms of growing the trees from which it is made, and converting those trees into paper, has an environmental impact that includes issues like

- deforestation and sustainability
- water consumption, conservation and pollution
- energy consumption and conservation

which pulp and paper producers, printers and publishers are trying to reduce, partly through economic self-interest, partly because of consumer pressure, partly because of a growing awareness of the environmental issues, and partly because of an increasing sense of corporate social responsibility.

These issues are now the concern of global organisations like the Forest Stewardship Council (FSC) and the Programme for the Endorsement of Forest Certification (PEFC), non-profit, non-governmental organisations (NGOs) that have been set up specifically to develop and promote standards for sustainable forest management and chain of custody certification, both of which make it easier for businesses to identify and know where they are buying their raw materials from, and to make responsible decisions based on this knowledge.

However, as the FSC website makes clear, their concern is not limited to trees:

> The intent of the FSC system is to shift the market to eliminate habitat destruction, water pollution, displacement of indigenous peoples and violence against people and wildlife that often accompanies logging.
>
> (www.fscus.org/paper)

Their work is complemented by a range of consumer initiatives at national level, like the British publishers' Environmental Action Group (EAG) and PREPS (the Publishers' Database for Responsible Environmental Paper Sourcing), which involves 23 British publishers, who have created a database of the pulps and forest sources used by their members, and also use the paper grading system created by the publishers Egmont UK and environmental consultants Ancona, based on a star system to classify papers according to whether the pulp from which they are made has been legally harvested or recycled, and the ways in which the forest sources are managed.

At the top of the list are 5-star papers, which are certified by FSC as being pure, mixed or recycled, and whose forest sources have received an FSC Forest Management licence. Egmont and PREPS members will only buy 3-star paper or higher. 1- or 2-star papers, those where there is not enough data to identify their forest source, or where there is reason to suspect that they are from an unwanted source, are not used.

Printers are also involved in these initiatives, and increasing numbers are able to display the FSC chain of custody (CoC) certification logo on their products, which makes it easier for publishers to produce green products.

## Recycled paper

Recycled paper is made from recycled fibre from waste paper, and the source of this is either pre-consumer or post-consumer waste.

Pre-consumer waste is paper that has not been used, and the main sources are from the conversion process when giant reels of paper, weighing several tonnes each, are slit into sheets, or into smaller reels for web printing; and from paper that has been rejected or damaged during paper making. These sources are known as 'mill broke', and are not considered true waste.

Post-consumer waste comes from three sources:

- printers' waste – printed or unprinted – such as trimmings, spoilt sheets, spoiled reels or rejects
- domestic or office waste – printed or unprinted
- news stand returns.

Because it is difficult to establish recycled fibre content, some recycled paper suppliers operate a system for classifying the fibre content of their papers:

- A – mill broke, which cannot be used in products labelled as recycled
- B – wood-free unprinted waste, mainly from converters
- C – wood-free printed waste
- D – mechanical pulp printed waste.

In this system, for example, a paper described as 40C/60D is made up of 40 per cent wood-free printed waste, and 60 per cent mechanical.

Recycled paper must contain a minimum of 50 per cent of a combination of fibres from all three sources for it to carry the British National Association of Paper Merchants (NAPM) recycled logo. Recycled paper certified by FSC also carries the FSC logo.

From an environmental point of view, the higher the post-consumer waste content the better. For every tonne of 100 per cent post-consumer recycled paper used instead of virgin pulp, the following savings can be made:

*Table* 5.6 Savings made

| | |
|---|---|
| Trees saved | 21 |
| Energy saved | 3,836.7kWh |
| Carbon dioxide reduced | 428kg |
| Solid waste reduced | 760kg |

in addition to savings in air pollution through emissions, and water pollution through water-borne waste.

From a publishing or printing perspective a recycled paper's fitness for purpose, as well as its printability and runnability, need to be considered when choosing one for a specific job.

However, it is worth noting that, over the past five years, the quality of recycled papers has improved a great deal, to the point that today's recycled papers are a match for their virgin fibre equivalents on price and availability, as well as on brightness, opacity, bulk and finish. They also run well on press, do not tear, pick or cause linting. Most printers, especially those with FSC certification, are happy to supply and use them.

# Inks

Printing inks come in two broad types – mineral-oil (petroleum) based and vegetable-oil based (vegetable inks).

Whatever their source, they need to possess certain basic characteristics that make them suited for use on high speed sheet- or web-fed offset presses.

These characteristics are:

- a high degree of tack (or stickiness) so that they adhere to the paper during printing
- a high concentration of pigment to produce a strong colour
- an ability to dry quickly so they do not smudge when handled, or set off onto paper stacked above and below.

Offset printing ink comes as a paste. It looks rather like decorator's paint, and is made up of three basic components:

- pigment
- vehicle
- additives.

The *pigment* gives ink its defining colour and opacity. The *vehicle,* besides giving ink its viscosity and flow, holds the pigment in suspension, and binds it to the paper. The ingredients in the vehicle vary according to the printing method – cold-set offset, heat-set offset – and the type of paper.

The *additives*, which are mainly chemical, act as:

- *dryers*, for accelerated drying (for example, salts or soaps of cobalt, manganese, zirconium, vanadium)
- *extenders*, for increased coverage (for example, barium sulphate)
- *anti-oxidants*, to prevent the ink from drying out on the press and forming a skin (for example, hydroquinone).

The amount of each these ingredients varies to produce an ink suited to the printing method and paper it is being printed on.

## Ink drying

Once the ink has been transferred to the paper it has to cure (go hard) and then dry. How quickly this happens depends on the:

- formulation of the ink
- drying process
- nature of the paper.

Ink can dry in a number of ways:

- Absorption (or penetration): ink penetrates the paper fibres, and is absorbed by them. The depth of penetration determines how quickly the ink dries. This is a relatively slow process, and is mainly used in cold-set offset printing.
- Oxidation: oxygen in the air combines with the vehicle to convert it from its liquid into a solid state. The process is accelerated by a catalyst, so that the ink dries quickly. Mainly used in sheet-fed offset printing.
- Evaporation: solvents in the vehicle are evaporated by heat to bind the pigment to the substrate. This method is used in gravure printing, but can also be used in heat-set web offset printing.
- Polymerisation, or radiation: used with ultraviolet (UV) inks, which harden when exposed to radiation from UV light, or electron beam (EB), and heat from infrared (IR) heaters.

### Inks and the environment

Petroleum-based printing inks, because of their ingredients, have a relatively high environmental impact. They contain pigments and oils which need to be extracted from the earth, and solvents that emit volatile organic compounds (VOCs) into the air, which cause air pollution, and are harmful to health.

Over the past twenty years, ink manufacturers have put a lot of money and effort into producing inks with a lower environmental impact, and this has led to the development, and increasing adoption by printers, of vegetable-oil based inks (vegetable inks), produced from bio-derived, renewable sources such as soy, safflower, cotton seed and canola.

Although their VOC emission rate is negligible, vegetable inks, like their petroleum-based equivalents, still have to meet the demands of high speed printing. For this, they need to have high tack, dry quickly and deliver strong colours; and this means that they contain virtually the same pigments and additives as petroleum-based inks.

Although vegetable inks are becoming more widely accepted, they do take longer to dry than petroleum-based inks, because they contain little (if any) VOC-emitting solvents, and this makes them difficult to use on coated stock.

It is certainly worth looking into the use of vegetable inks wherever possible, especially if you, or your company, are trying to reduce the size of your carbon footprint.

Nevertheless, even vegetable inks come at an environmental cost, in their case associated with the fact that they come from resources that have to be planted (sometimes at the expense of the surrounding habitat, as is the case with soy production in the Amazon rain forest), tended and harvested.

A really radical look at your products and how you produce them, might lead you to consider:

- reducing format sizes (smaller formats use less ink, as well as less paper)
- reducing the areas of ink coverage – for example, dark solids and bled pages
- changing to digital printing (though this, too, has an environmental cost!).

## Adhesives

Adhesives, or glues, are used in bookbinding to join the pages or signatures of a book together in perfect, as well as in notch, slotted or burst binding. They are also used to join the various pieces of the case together, as well as the book block to the case, in hardback binding.

Modern adhesives have been formulated so that they:

- dry quickly
- bond strongly
- are able to retain shape
- are flexible
- are durable
- can withstand stress and long periods in storage.

How effective they are is judged by their performance in the bound book, using the following criteria:

- page-pull strength: how strongly a page remains attached to the spine of a bound book
- lie flat: the book's ability to lie flat and stay open at a given page
- easy open: the ease with which a book opens on first opening
- spine flexibility: the ability of the book's spine to withstand wrinkling, creasing and cracking after repeated opening.

Although there are hundreds of adhesives to choose from, they come in three types, each one based on the chemistry of different ethylene polymers, homopolymers and copolymers:

- water-based emulsions (also known as cold-melts), are based on polyvinyl acetate (PVAc) homopolymers, or vinyl acetate ethylene (VAE) copolymers.
- hot-melts, are based on ethylene vinyl acetate (EVA) copolymers.
- reactive hot-melts (also known as warm-melts), are based on solid pre-polymer polyurethanes or PURs.

### *Water-based emulsion adhesives (VAE) and (PVAc)*

Of the two water-based emulsions, VAEs are the preferred choice because of their natural flexibility. PVAc tends to dry brittle, and runs the risk of cracking, rather like conventional hot-melts.

Water-based VAE-based emulsions are used for the first shot in two-shot perfect binding. Because of their water content they are good at penetrating paper, and quickly develop the strong bond needed to hold everything – pages and cover – together.

They:

- allow the book to lie flat
- allow the book to open easily
- do not crack in extreme cold
- are the most durable of all adhesive bindings
- are flexible
- retain shape, and are particularly useful for case bound books which have a rounded spine.

However, they:

- are slow to dry
- have a relatively low page-pull strength
- do not work successfully with coated papers.

Generally speaking, this type of adhesive is not used for perfect binding, where speed and low cost are essential.

### Hot-melt adhesives (EVA)

Hot-melt adhesives need to have waxes and resins added to them to make them less rigid and more flexible.

Hot-melt EVAs, with these waxes and resins:

- allow the book to lie flat
- allow the book to open easily
- do not crack in cold conditions
- have a high page-pull strength
- are flexible.

They also:

- dry quickly
- can be used with a wide range of paper stocks – uncoated and coated.

However, their high application temperature can cause paper warping, especially in cross-grained paper.

This type of adhesive is suited to perfect binding, where speed and low cost are critical.

### Hot-melt adhesives (PUR)

PUR-based adhesives are a relatively recent arrival on the bookbinding scene.

They:

- allow the book to lie flat
- allow the book to open easily

- do not crack in cold conditions
- have a very high page-pull strength
- are more flexible than EVA adhesives
- retain shape.

They also:

- produce a very strong bond
- work well with any kind of paper stock
- are applied at a lower temperature than EVA-based hot-melts, so do not cause paper warping.

In early versions of PUR hot-melts drying time was relatively slow, and it could take as much as 24 hours before finished books could be handled. However, recent developments have produced PUR hot-melts that dry almost as fast as EVA hot-melts.

PUR hot-melts can be up to three times more expensive to buy than conventional EVA hot-melts, though the amount needed is about half that used in conventional EVA hot-melt work.

## Coatings: lamination and varnishing

Most covers and jackets are now laminated or varnished after printing (off-press) to give them protection against wear and tear: scuffing, scratches and fingermarks (which can be a real problem with heavy solids, especially blues), and to make them look attractive when displayed.

Lamination is done by bonding a thin transparent film laminate to the entire cover or jacket. The film comes in thicknesses between 11 and 19 microns (thousandths of a millimetre), and is made from oriented polypropylene (OPP), which is more flexible and robust than other types of laminate. The most commonly used thickness is 12 microns.

Laminates come in a range of finishes from matt to glossy.

Although cover board is already quite strong because it is thick, both it, and much thinner jacket paper, benefit from the extra strength that comes from being laminated.

Some colours, especially blues and some reds, have a tendency, over time, to bleed into the laminate in reversed out work. If you are thinking of using this range of colours, it might be worth discussing this with your supplier.

A cheaper form of coating is varnish, and three types are available.

Ultraviolet (UV) varnish. This is applied as a liquid to the cover or jacket, and then cured by UV radiation. UV varnish produces a hard, high gloss finish, but does not provide the same strength as lamination.

UV varnish can be used either to cover the entire cover or jacket, or as a spot coating in combination with a matt laminate, to highlight parts of the design.

Less expensive than UV varnish, and often used as an alternative, is nitrocellulose (NC) varnish, which is dried by heat to produce a high gloss finish.

Finally, there is machine varnish, which is applied on-press, and is mainly used as a sealant for heavy solids. The finish is less high gloss than UV or NC varnish, but it is effective in protecting the cover or jacket from wear.

## Coverings: cloth – imitation and real

The binding case used in hardback binding is made up of the front and back boards and the spine hollow. These are covered and held together by material known generically as a covering.

The covering can either be leather, real (woven) cloth, plastic or paper which has been printed and embossed to look like woven cloth, and is known as imitation cloth.

### Imitation cloth

The most commonly used covering is imitation cloth, known by a number of trade names most of which end with *-lin*. This is because most imitation cloths are embossed, very convincingly, to look like linen, though they do come in a number of different finishes.

There are a lot of colours to choose from, and you do this using a swatch which shows the different colours and finishes. The weight of imitation cloths starts at 105gsm, and goes up to 155gsm for heavier books, or where strength is needed.

Imitation cloths are relatively inexpensive.

### Real cloth

If you are looking for strength and durability, you might consider using a real cloth, though real cloths are more expensive than imitation cloths.

Real cloths are made from cotton. The least expensive are the white backs, so-called because only their outer surface is coloured, the inner surface (or back) being left white. They are sturdy and durable.

At the top of the range in terms of strength and durability, as well as cost, come library buckram and crash canvas.

### Leather

Leather is the most expensive form of covering, and most often used to confer a certain cachet to a particular product: a presentation binding, for example. It can only be worked by hand, and as such does not lend itself to mass production, unlike the other forms of covering.

Not surprisingly, there is a whole host of leathers to choose from: goat (also known as morocco, and the most expensive), pig, skiver (sheep), cow and calf (also known as vellum), all of which serve a variety of needs, and make it essential for you to discuss this kind of work with the person who is going to carry it out.

*Plastic*

Plastic, mainly vinyls, can be used as a covering, and is useful where the book may be exposed to damp – for example, a botanical field guide or a book on sailing. However, lamination is equally effective, and a lot cheaper.

Plastic also has a tendency to keep its 'memory' and return to its original shape. This causes cases to lose their shoulders and joints, which is rather unsightly. This, together with the fact that it is difficult to block, is reason enough to use plastic as a covering only when it is absolutely unavoidable.

*Blocking foils*

Metallic blocking is used on the case to show the book's title and the name of the author. It is also used on covers and jackets to highlight parts of the design, and make the book look more attractive and noticeable.

Foils are most commonly imitation gold or silver, but a lot of other colours are available.

Gold leaf is also available but, because of its expense, it is generally reserved for books bound in leather.

We have now come to the end of the chapter on raw materials. Choosing raw materials is not inherently that difficult. The real difficulty lies in choosing the right raw materials for the job in terms of fitness for purpose and budget. It is to be hoped that reading this chapter will make this easier, if not more enjoyable. But remember, if all else fails, you can always discuss things with the supplier.

# 6 Printing

We have now reached a fork in the road along which our content has been travelling. It can either stay in its virtual form and take a digital route to make its appearance as pixels on the screen of a computer or an ereader; or it can take the route that leads to its appearance in print as ink or toner on paper.

In this chapter, we shall be looking at the options available to you to produce your work, in terms of the technologies, the presses and the processes.

Let's start by looking at the technology, of which there are several to choose from:

- offset lithography
- digital
- letterpress
- gravure.

Although these all have their uses in book printing, the two predominant technologies for book work are offset lithography (which I shall call litho for short) and digital. Which of these two to choose is going to depend as much on the nature of your job as its cost, what you are trying to achieve and whether the book is front list or back list.

## Litho and digital printing

Litho printing and digital printing both produce books as the end product, but how they do this is very different.

A digital press works on the same principle as a desktop printer, and transfers the image to the paper, usually a page at a time, using toner (with a laser printer) or water-based ink (with an inkjet printer). Like your desktop printer, it takes virtually no time to set up a job: there are no plates and there is no make ready. With an in-line perfect binding facility, it is possible to produce a single, perfect bound copy of an 800-page single-colour book with a 4-colour cover in less than a minute. This makes digital printing *the* technology for single copy (print on demand) and short-run printing for up to 350–400 copies – the optimum number being dictated more by the economics of the project, than the logistics.

In litho printing the image is first transferred to a printing plate, and ultimately to the paper using ink. Pages are usually printed in groups of 4, 8 or 16 at a time. So, for example, a 320-page book, printed in groups of 8-pages will need 40 plates. Each of these has to be processed before it can be used for printing, and each one needs to be made ready on the press to make sure it prints properly.

Once printed, the pages then have to be bound and finished, either with a cover if the book is a paperback, or with a case if it is a hardback.

All of this takes time, and it is impossible to produce stock at anything like the speed of digital printing.

Nevertheless, both technologies offer features and benefits that the other cannot, and at the moment they manage to exist happily side by side. However, with the ever-continuing and rapid developments taking place in the digital world and the publishing industry, how much longer this will continue to be the case remains to be seen, especially with the latest developments in inkjet printing.

## Digital printing – print on demand and digital web

### Benefits

Digital printing offers a number of important benefits that make it particularly attractive to the publisher. To begin with, having effectively no set-up time or costs, digital printing is capable of producing books on demand in very small quantities, very quickly.

Being able to produce books in this way has virtually eliminated the risk (and cost) which comes with producing books in quantities which, at best, can only be an educated guess, and of having to store (and possibly waste) stock that may never sell. So much so, that some publishers now choose to print the first run of a new title digitally, either in small quantities; or, in the more radical business model, by publishing first on the web and printing and distributing digitally produced copies later on demand.

When it comes to the back list, titles need no longer go out of print. Instead, they can be stored and reprinted digitally to order, providing a hitherto undreamt of income stream. An example of this is Cambridge University Press' 'Lazarus Project' which has brought 13,000 out-of-print titles back to life (Cambridge University Press, June 2011).

Finally, because data in digital printing is dynamic and flexible, it is possible to produce personalised books. This certainly has its uses in educational publishing from primary school right through to university, from basic readers to advanced textbooks. One interesting use of digital print can be seen in photo-personalised books, particularly in children's books, where a person ordering a book supplies names and photographs of faces for the characters appearing in a story.

### Limitations

However, (for the moment at least) digital printing does have some limitations, mainly to do with cost and quality.

*Cost*

When a digital book is being printed and bound it is treated as a complete job, and the next book is treated as a new job. If you are producing ten different titles digitally one after the other, this makes sense. But, if you are producing 500 copies of the same book this way, you do not get the economies of scale that you would get if you were to print using digital web or litho, as can be seen from the case study below. In itself, this is not necessarily a reason not to use digital printing when your print run starts to grow: perhaps it is the only way you can produce the book, in which case cost is not an issue. But where cost *is* an issue, you will need to explore the costs of printing litho.

There is a point (known as the crossover point) at which digital web and litho printing are more economical than print on demand; but where this occurs changes from job to job, as it depends entirely on circumstances.

## Case study 6.1

In this case study the specification was sent to a POD printer, who also quoted for producing the same book using a digital web press and a litho press.

Trimmed page size: 216 x 138mm (Demy 8vo; portrait)
Extent: 320 pages
Text to be printed black ink only throughout from PDF files supplied, on an 80gsm white offset paper.
Binding: unsewn, cover 4 scored/side glued, cut flush
Cover: 4/0 from PDF files supplied, on a 240gsm single-sided board; laminated 12 micron OPP laminate
Delivery to a single address: Extra

*Table 6.1* Comparison of prices between POD, digital web and litho printing

| Process | Quantity | Price | 100 run on |
|---|---|---|---|
| POD | 1 | £3.80 | - |
|  | 10 | £38.00 | - |
|  | 350 | £1330.00 |  |
| Digital web | 350 | £663.00 | £120.50 |
|  | 700 | £1085.00 | £120.50 |
|  | 1000 | £1446.50 | £120.50 |
|  | 1500 | £2049.00 | £120.50 |
| Litho | 350 | £979.00 | £90.20 |
|  | 700 | £1294.70 | £90.20 |
|  | 1000 | £1565.30 | £90.20 |
|  | 1500 | £2016.30 | £90.20 |

As the figures show, digital web printing is capable of producing books very economically, with unit costs for 350 copies (at £1.89 per copy) considerably lower than can be achieved by either POD (£3.80) a copy and litho (£2.80), making it a powerful alternative to litho.

The speed with which digital printers are able to work depends on a number of factors, and the main one is, understandably, standardisation. Nowhere is this more apparent than when it comes to paper and binding, where choice is restricted:

- paper is likely to be offered in two weights and two shades – for example, a natural shade 80gsm M/F book wove, or a white shade 75sgm M/F book wove
- books are usually perfect bound paperbacks, or saddle-stitched; though perfect bound hardbacks can also be produced

The extent is not a problem; and most formats can be catered for.

For some these limitations may be one limitation too far. But when you take into account the fact that you can supply a single copy of an out-of-print book to a customer within two working days, it may be a small price to pay. The product is fit for purpose.

However, when it comes to 4-colour work, there are still some reservations in people's minds about this when it comes to digital printing. This may have been justifiable five years ago, as digital colour printing was still in its infancy, and common causes for complaint were that:

- the final product looked dull
- the image lacked punch
- the paper was not suitable.

But, digital colour printing has improved a great deal recently with the introduction of a new generation of sophisticated laser and inkjet printers capable of producing good quality work that compares very well with work produced by litho.

## Litho printing

Despite all the advantages that come with printing digitally, litho printing is still the preferred technology when it comes to producing a quality product with high production values: for instance, an art book, where the quality of the printing and the paper are important market considerations.

As shown in the case study, litho wins on price when it comes to print runs above 1500 copies – though, even as this is being written, the latest generation of inkjet printers is nibbling away at this, raising the crossover point at which litho becomes economic to as high as 5,000 copies.

Above 5,000 copies, litho comes into its own in terms of quality, cost and its ability to produce relatively large numbers of printed pages quickly.

## Which technology? Making the final choice

At either end of the scale it is fairly easy to decide which technology to use for your job: single-copy and short-run jobs are natural candidates for digital printing, just as long-run jobs, or a job where quality is paramount, are natural candidates for litho printing. It is around the crossover point that the choice gets difficult. Because of this, it is essential to discuss the job with the supplier to get as much information as possible before you decide one way or the other.

In the end, though, it is your decision; and that should be based on three criteria:

- fitness for purpose
- how long it will take
- what you are prepared to pay.

## The presses

Litho printing is either sheet-fed or web-fed.

### Sheet-fed presses

Sheet-fed presses take a sheet of blank paper in at one end and produce a printed sheet at the other.

Printing speeds, or the number of impressions per hour (iph), vary from job to job, but a good average speed is about 12,000 iph, dropping with the complexity of the job and the weight and type of paper – for example, 1,500 iph or lower for a lightweight (37gsm) bible paper.

Litho presses come in a range of sizes and configurations to suit all kinds of work, from single-sided, single-colour to double-sided 4-colour.

For double-sided single-colour work the best press for the job is a perfector press, which delivers a sheet printed on both sides.

For 4-colour process work printers are moving away from single-sided 4-colour presses to 5- and even 6-colour perfectors. By using a 6-colour perfector you can:

- print in four colours on both sides of the sheet
- print an extra colour on both sides of the sheet
- seal the colours in on both sides of the sheet.

Or you could have two extra colours on either side of the sheet if you did not want to seal the colours.

For work involving spot (or Pantone Matching System [PMS]) colours, it is best to discuss the job with the supplier, as there is a wide range of press configurations to choose from. For example, you might find it cheaper to print spot colours as 4-colour process, though the final results may not be as consistent or as faithful as they might have been had you printed them as true spot colours, which might be an important consideration when it comes to company or corporate colours.

In the end, it is essential, if you want to end up with a good quality product, to make sure that the job is printed on the machine designed to do that kind of work.

Of course, it *is* possible to print your job on any kind of press, and this may even be necessary if there is no suitable alternative. But it makes little sense in terms of cost, time, wastage, quality and general effort to print a double-sided 4-colour job on a single-sided single-colour press, when the right equipment is available.

### Web-fed presses

Web-fed presses print onto a continuous reel of paper, known as a web. The blank web is fed into the press at one end, and it comes out of the press as a folded section, printed on both sides.

Printing speeds are high when compared with litho presses, starting at 16,000 iph and going up to 40,000 iph, depending on the nature of the work.

Web presses come in a variety of sizes, but the range of formats they can offer is limited by the cut-off (the size of the plate cylinder) on the one hand, and the folding mechanism on the other.

Web printing is still used a lot for long-run printing, especially colour work. Its main advantages over litho are its speed, and the fact that it delivers folded sections.

However, as already mentioned, they offer a limited number of formats, they take longer to make ready than a litho press, paper wastage can be higher than for litho and you may end up with short-grain sections.

There are two types of web press:

- heat set
- cold set.

Heat-set web presses are fitted with dryers, which dry the printed paper as it passes through the press. This makes it possible to print on papers with low absorbency, such as art paper, or offset cartridge. Heat-set web presses are mainly used for colour work.

Cold-set web presses don't have dryers, so the ink on the paper has to dry by absorption or penetration. Cold-set web printing is best suited to long-run mass-market paperback printing, or monochrome printing on absorbent paper.

The determining factor between sheet-fed and web-fed litho is the size of the print run. If you are in mass-market paperback publishing a lot of your work will most likely be produced on webs. If you are an educational publisher producing long runs of 4-colour textbooks on coated stock, then, again, web printing is probably the choice for you. If you publish art books, where quantities are small, say, 3,500–5,000, then sheet-fed is probably the best option. Ten, even five, years ago the choices, and the reasons for making those choices, were quite clear cut. However, as already mentioned, new developments in printing technology, and a trend amongst publishers towards shorter print runs, make it much harder to make the right choice. If issues of costs or quality are difficult to reconcile, the best people to talk to are the printers themselves.

## Litho monochrome and colour printing

### *Monochrome printing: black and white line work*

Monochrome, or single-colour, printing is generally taken to mean printing in black and white, and large quantities of work are printed this way, especially books for the trade, or consumer, market. Strictly speaking, though, monochrome means one colour, which means that it can be any single colour: red or brown for instance. In view of this, it is good practice to specify the colour, even if it is only black, rather than assuming that the printer will instinctively know this.

Monochrome printing can be on one or both sides of the sheet. This is written as 1/0 (spoken: 'one back zero') for single-sided printing, and 1/1 (one back one) for double-sided printing.

For colours other than black, either used for monochrome printing or for spot printing, where you are adding an additional colour to the black working, the only way to identify and specify colour is to use a colour matching system like the Pantone Matching System (PMS), which identifies colours by numbers, which are standard round the world. So, for example, PMS 1395 means the same thing to a printer in the UK as it does to one in China or Spain. For complete accuracy you should specify your colours from a printed swatch rather than from a computer screen. This is because colours on a screen vary according to the graphics card and screen calibration of your computer.

### *Monochrome printing: black and white halftone illustrations*

The term monochrome halftone illustration is generally used to describe a black and white photograph, which has gradations of colour in it, ranging from black to dark grey (called shadows), through grey to light grey (midtones) to pure white (highlights). Where the image is pure black the black ink prints as a solid, and ink coverage is 100 per cent. To reproduce the greys and the whites in the rest of the image, the same black ink that printed the solid blacks has to be broken up. This is done by transforming anything in the image that is not a solid into a series of dots. These dots transfer the ink onto the paper, and they vary in size according to the intensity of the light in the image: for shadows the dot sizes range from 70 to 100 per cent, mid-tones from 30 to 70 per cent, and highlights from 0 to 30 per cent. So, the darker the image, the bigger the dot and the more ink, the lighter the image the smaller the dot and the less ink, to the point that where there is no dot there is no ink either, like, for example, a white shirt on a sunny day, where the whiteness of the shirt comes from the whiteness of the paper.

### Colour printing: spot colour

Spot printing is used to add an extra colour to a black-printed sheet to highlight text or part of an image, and is most often found in educational books and manuals, where instructions and diagrams can be easier to understand if another colour is used.

The same convention is used to describe whether the sheet is printed single- or double-sided, and the number of inks. So, a double-sided sheet printed in black ink with the same spot colour on both sides would be described as 'printed 2/2 in black with one spot colour PMS 123.'

The inks (colours) used in spot printing are already mixed before they are used for printing. So, a green ink looks green, and prints green. It is not possible to create a green by printing a PMS blue on top of a PMS yellow: all you will get is a mess. So, spot colours do not behave like process colours, where overprinting a yellow with blue (cyan) does produce green.

Spot colours are usually printed in one shade as a solid, in which case ink coverage is 100 per cent. However, it is possible to break a solid spot colour up to produce different shades, ranging from dark to light. This is done by using a tint, which is an evenly spaced array of horizontal and vertical dots all of the same size that transfer the ink to the paper. Densities start at 90 per cent and go down, in steps of 10 per cent, to 70 per cent for shadows, from 70 to 30 per cent for midtones, and from 30 to 0 per cent for highlights.

For example, from a solid red (PMS 185), it is possible to produce a dark red, a mid-red and a pink by laying a:

- 90 per cent tint for the dark red
- 60 per cent tint for the mid-red
- 50 per cent tint for the pink.

For a lighter pink, you would use a 30 per cent tint, or lower. Without a tint, this would have involved using four different spot colours:

- PMS 185 for the solid
- PMS 186 for the dark red
- PMS 192 for the mid-red
- PMS 189 for the pink.

However, this would be uneconomical and difficult to print.

Using tints allows you to vary the shade (or intensity) of a colour, but they cannot be used to create different hues (or colours) – for example, lime green and olive green. The only way to do this is to use two different PMS colours: PMS 369 and PMS 385, in the same way that you would have to use two different PMS colours to produce a red or a blue. Deciding to use different colours, rather than going for different shades, may be an essential part of the design, but it does add to the cost of printing – for example, a black working + 1 spot colour is a 2-colour job. By adding an extra colour it becomes a 3-colour job, and so on.

## 4-colour printing

4-colour printing, like monochrome printing, allows different configurations. The most common one is when the sheet is printed in four colours on both sides of the sheet – 4/4 (four back four). Some publishers use a 4/1 combination, where the sheet is printed in four colours on one side, and black only on the reverse. When the sheet is folded, every other double page spread is 4-colour, those in between being black. Clearly, this combination needs careful planning at the design stage to make sure that illustrations that need to be in colour appear on the pages to be printed in colour.

Colour printing handles line and halftone work with equal ease, making it unnecessary to distinguish between the two.

4-colour printing uses four inks only – cyan (blue), magenta (red), yellow and key (black) – and for this reason this kind of printing is often referred to as CMYK printing.

4-colour inks, also known as process inks, are made with transparent pigments, which make it possible for another colour to be produced when the inks are combined during printing. For example:

- cyan and magenta combined = violet/purple
- magenta and yellow combined = orange
- cyan and yellow combined = green
- cyan, magenta and yellow combined = black.

Cyan, magenta and yellow are subtractive primary colours, so-called because they subtract (or absorb) some light waves and reflect others. To do this best, subtractive colours need to be able to subtract colours from a substrate which reflects light to its maximum potential; and the best one for this is considered to be white coated paper. If you print on an ivory paper, or a paper with a yellow cast to it, the colours will become distorted and unable to reproduce the original faithfully.

The opposite of subtractive primaries are additive primaries: red, green and blue (RGB). These work with emitted light, rather than pigments, and, when added together in equal amounts, create white light. They are familiar from their use in television and computer screens.

Colour images, like monochrome images, need to be broken down into half-tone dots before they can be printed. They also need to be separated into the four colours.

As with monochrome halftone printing, there are shadows, midtones and highlights. The overall brightness and lift of the image depends on the whiteness of the paper. To see this, take a strong magnifying glass (sometimes called a linen tester) and look at a printed image, where there are, say, some clouds or some snow. You will see there are virtually no halftone dots there at all; or, if there are any, they will be minute. The whiteness and brightness of the snow or the clouds come from how white and bright the paper is.

To create different shades of colour the halftone dots of varying sizes combine to form small rosettes that produce the desired colour in the right strength. So, for example, for a mid-green, medium-sized cyan dots need to combine with medium-sized yellow dots.

Looking at the dots under a magnifying glass shows you how the mechanics of 4-colour printing work. Actually turning all these dots into a seamless colour picture is something that your eyes do for you. In short, the experience of looking at a printed colour image depends as much on your subconscious responses as it does on the printer's conscious attempts to make the image appear at its best.

### Matching the original

In monochrome printing it is quite possible, with a bit of care, to produce a printed version of an image which is virtually indistinguishable from the original. This is because the printer is dealing with one ink only, and it is relatively simple to control. When it comes to colour printing, matters become more complex. Instead of one ink, there are now four, all working in combination across the sheet, with the added complication that pages are imposed in line, or in track. So, on a sheet printed 16-pages to view the pages will be imposed in a pattern of 4 pages across and 4 pages down. Pages in each column are said to be in track, or in line, with each other.

This creates a problem with ink balance when a page in a column needs more ink than another. To take a simple example, two of the pages in track 1 have a lot of yellow in them, one has a lot of blue in it and the last has a lot of red in it. If the printer decides to increase the supply of yellow ink so that the yellow pages match the strength of the yellow in the original (and the proofs), the blue in the blue page will start to change to green, and the red on the red page to orange. The skill of the printer is to achieve a colour balance that satisfies, as far as is possible, the colour requirements of *all* the pages, and the only way to do that is by compromise.

When you check 4-colour printed output, you need to remember this, and you should look at the finished product for what it looks like in its own right, and not in comparison with proofs, or the originals. Proofs are essentially for checking the quality of the scanning; but, because they have been produced under very different conditions from the main run, where pages are printed in track and at high speeds, they are not reliable for checking the quality of work from the main run.

You need also to bear in mind the journey that the original image has had to make to reappear as a printed image on a sheet of paper. For litho printing, that picture with its palette of hundreds of different colours and shades has been:

- scanned and reduced to a series of halftone dots in four separate colours
- transferred to four printing plates
- transferred from the printing plates to the blanket
- transferred from the blanket to the paper (or substrate).

Only when it reaches the paper is it reunited to become an image again; and, as we know, even then it is only an intricate grid of different sized spots of colour, which have combined to look like the original.

Knowing this, makes it easier to understand why the colours in your 4-colour job might not be able to match exactly the colours in the original, and that what you have got is as close an approximation as the printer can manage, given the nature of the processes and the raw materials involved.

An interesting exercise is to go to a bookshop and to compare books containing identical images but produced by different publishers. The best books for this are art books. Find two or three books on the same artist, museum or exhibition, find three examples of the same picture and compare their colour values. By now, it should come as no surprise that they will vary quite considerably.

Each publisher has been faced with the factors described above, and each one has had to make the decision that their product is of an acceptable quality.

But this is only one aspect of quality. In the section below we cover the other aspects of quality you, and the printer, should be checking. If your job has been printed without any of these defects, then you can be sure that your product is good quality and fit for purpose.

## Managing quality: inspection and control

Managing the quality of the product is a process that continues throughout the project. It starts during the planning phase when the specification was first drawn up, and continues at specific points during the development and production phases when we are given opportunities to check that the quality of the output from one process is good enough for it to become the input for the next process, and to put things right if they are not of an acceptable quality.

Up to now, we have been dealing with content, which exists in a virtual environment as something unique and intangible. This all changes when we start printing, and produce multiple physical copies, which we are going to take to market. Now is the time to check the quality of what has been printed, before it is turned into a bound book.

In the case of print on demand and digital short-run printing, there is virtually no opportunity to carry out checks on quality. This is because stock is printed, bound and dispatched in what amounts to a single operation. Interrupting the workflow to check quality is not an option, as it would slow it down and defeat the object of these production models – rapid fulfilment of orders.

For other work, where speed is not a critical factor, it is perfectly possible to interrupt the workflow to check the quality of output, and the first opportunity to do so is when printing has been completed, and the printer either supplies the publisher with a set of folded and trimmed printed sheets (known as running sheets), which should be taken at random from the print run, so that they are representative of the job as a whole, and have not been selected because they are the best; or they make it possible for the publisher to check printed output electronically, which can be done by email or by allowing the publisher access to their website to check printed output there. Although checking proofs electronically doesn't allow you to *see* the actual printing, doing it this way cuts down on the time (and effort) that would otherwise be taken getting the running sheets to the publisher.

This is the publisher's chance to check that there are no problems with the:

- paper
- printing
- design.

However, there is a growing trend amongst publishers not to check the quality of a supplier's work, as they consider that the responsibility for that, and for good printing lies with the supplier and not with the customer. They believe that it is enough for them to have chosen a good supplier and good raw materials, and that the risk of something going wrong, as well as the cost and effort of putting it right if this happens, should be borne by the supplier, and should not be shared by involving the customer in checking the quality of printed output, particularly when the supplier has been given accreditation for quality management, such as ISO 9001.

This is certainly transparent and leaves the supplier in no doubt about the terms under which they work for that publisher. It also saves time, since binding can start without having to wait for approval of the printed output from the publisher. However, not all suppliers are prepared to work this way, so this is something that needs to be discussed with them before you place the job.

If you do intend to inspect the quality of the printed output then now is the time, before binding starts, to spot any problems and have them put right. It is easier, quicker and cheaper to replace a problem sheet, or folded section, with a reprint of the affected sheet, than it is to try and have things put right once the book has been bound. In the case of a perfect bound paperback, it is virtually impossible to do this, and the only option is to destroy the faulty stock and start printing all over again.

## Inspection

As you check the running sheets, these are the things that you should be looking out for:

### Printing and paper defects

#### Wrong imposition

If the imposition is wrong the section will be folded so that the page numbers (folios) do not run in the correct sequence within the section. If you are using a printer-binder, where everything is done under one roof, the problem is unlikely to occur. It is most likely to occur when binding is being done by a trade binder. It is the binder who specifies the imposition scheme, and the printer needs to impose sheets accordingly.

#### Creasing

Creasing is caused by printing on paper that has not been conditioned properly. Paper must be allowed to adjust itself to the temperature and atmospheric conditions of the printing hall before it is used. If the paper is cold and the hall is warm, the paper will develop wavy edges. If the hall is cold and the paper is warm, it will develop tight edges. Both problems cause creasing.

#### Picking

Picking occurs mainly with coated papers and is caused when the strength of the ink tack pulls (picks) the coated surface off the base stock, leaving a white area in the middle of a print area. This is most likely to happen when the combined density of the ink per pixel in 4-colour printing exceeds 250 per cent, and can be controlled by grey component replacement (GCR).

#### Fluffing, linting, piling

Three terms which refer to the same problem, caused by the accumulation on the printing surface of loose fibres shed from the paper. Fluffing reduces the overall quality of the printing, and is most likely to occur in sheet-fed litho printing using papers which have not been surface-sized.

#### Hickey, doughnut

A hickey occurs when dried ink or debris attaches itself to the printing surface and leaves a blank, unprinted spot in a printed area. This type of hickey is a void hickey. A doughnut hickey is a ring of unprinted area, with a spot of ink in the middle.

## Printing defects

### Scumming

Ink appearing in the non-image areas of the page. This defect has a variety of causes, the most common of which is an over-acidic (or alkaline) fountain solution on the press, and adversely affects the chemistry of the printing plate.

### Mottle

Uneven printing in solid areas. The result either of poor quality ink, or uneven ink absorption by the paper.

### Slurring, doubling

Smearing or blurring of an image, mainly on the trailing edge, caused by problems on the press, such as:

- too much pressure between printing surfaces, or printing surfaces and paper
- a loose blanket, so that paper slips against it
- a blanket that is too soft
- an ink that is too soft
- too much ink, especially on a coated paper
- using defective paper, especially paper with wavy edges.

### Set off

The transfer of wet ink from the printed surface of a sheet to the back of the sheet that lies on top of it when it reaches the delivery tray immediately after it has been printed. It is likely to occur more frequently with heavier papers. However, the problem can be eliminated with the use of anti-set-off spray.

### Ghosting

The appearance of a ghost, or phantom, image on the printed side of the sheet. This is known as mechanical ghosting, and is caused either by ink starvation or by using incorrect diameter ink rollers. Ghosting on the reverse side of the printed sheet is known as chemical ghosting, and is caused by the ink on the sheet below reacting with the ink on the sheet above it and changing its drying properties. Chemical ghosting should not be confused with set off.

### Optical dot gain

The increase in size, by between 10 per cent and 35 per cent, of a halftone dot, during printing. The result of this is that shadows move towards solids, midtones move towards shadows, and highlights move towards midtones, so that the overall optical effect is darkened and detail is lost, especially in the shadow areas. The main cause of the problem is high paper porosity, but low ink viscosity can also be a factor.

It is perfectly possible to eliminate the effects of optical dot gain by reducing the size of the halftone during scanning, so that when it hits the paper it increases to the intended size. This is called dot gain compensation, and should be discussed with the person who is going to originate the halftones and the printer who is supplying the paper and printing the job.

### *Greyness, and colour variation*

Black text looks grey, and 4-colour printing lacks punch. The most common cause of this is an imbalance between water and ink on the press. This would normally have been picked up by the machine minder, who should be inspecting out-turn sheets, during printing.

Sometimes one side of the sheet is printed blacker than the other, and density may vary from section to section. To check that the black printing is consistently black throughout the book, look at the front and the back of a page in each section. If well printed, they should all be of the same density.

When checking colour work it is important to check colour consistency across double page spreads throughout the book. This is particularly important where two sections meet, and the left and right hand pages are not part of the same pass through the press. Consistency in colour work is critical, and marks the difference between acceptable and unacceptable colour printing. This is much more important than how closely the printed version matches the original.

### *Colour and tints out of register*

Register is the accurate positioning in relation to each other of the successive colours in colour printing, so that the image looks as though it is of one piece. Where register is inaccurate, printing is described as being out of register: images are blurred (so that they look like images for viewing through 3-D spectacles), and it is possible to see the four (or more) colours as separate colours. When tints are printed out of register they look blotchy.

## Design problems

At the same time as you are checking for problems with printing and paper, it is important to keep an eye out for design that seems not to be working. For example:

- a shade of colour that looked alright in proof may look weak when printed on the main run; this can be a problem, especially with yellows

- reversed-out type may be too small and too narrow, and has filled in, so that it is illegible
- an image may have been laterally reversed, and this has only just come to light.

Looking at the list of things that can go wrong, it might seem surprising that books ever get produced at all. However, when it comes down to it, most books are printed and bound without problems. This is because suppliers, more interested in prevention than cure, run their own quality management systems, and it is unusual for a problem to slip through the net to be discovered by you.

For your part, you have:

- chosen a supplier who, you believe, is capable of producing the quality of work you want
- defined the standards of that quality in a specification, and in discussion with the supplier
- chosen the right raw materials.

Nevertheless, things *can* sometimes go wrong; and when that happens, you need to know what to do.

## When something has gone wrong

The first thing to do is to get in touch with the supplier to tell them that there is a problem with the printing, and to ask them to let you know how much of the print run is affected.

Once you know the scope of the problem, you are in a better position to consider what is to be done next. However, before you can do this you need to find the answers to a number of questions that have a bearing on what you finally decide to do, and include the following.

- What is the nature of the problem?
- Is it major, or relatively minor?
- How much time is there left in the schedule to put the problem right?
- How, and to what degree, does the problem affect the quality of the finished product?
- How noticeable would it be to the purchaser, or reader?
- Would it be possible to leave the problem as it is, and refund money to dissatisfied customers instead?
- If the job has been printed on specially made paper is there enough left on which to reprint the affected section(s)?
- How and why did the problem occur; and who is responsible?
- How much will it cost to reprint the affected section(s)?
- Who is going to pay for all this?

Armed with answers to these questions, it should be possible to make a properly informed decision that deals sensibly and fairly with the situation, and allows the project to move forward.

## Printing and the environment

The printing industry uses a considerable amount of chemicals, raw materials and energy to create its products, and inevitably, this has an impact on the environment in the form of:

- water and air pollution
- waste
- carbon emissions.

One serious environmental impact associated with printing is the release into the atmosphere of volatile organic compounds (VOCs). VOCs are carbon-based compounds, such as acetone, isopropyl alcohol (IPA) and white spirit, which evaporate easily into the air, and are known to cause respiratory, allergic and immunological problems. VOCs occur in products used by printers in a range of activities which include:

- colour proofing
- plate processing
- cylinder preparation
- printing inks
- fountain solutions
- press washes
- cleaning solutions.

However, this situation is starting to change, driven by a number of factors:

- regulation to control the way industry, including the printing industry, manages itself and its environmental impact
- technological developments, which make it possible to do things differently
- increased public awareness.

As a result, printers have started to introduce environmental management systems (EMS) to help manage their company's environmental impact by measuring consumption and reducing waste, not only in terms of how they operate as an organisation, but also in terms of how they manufacture and distribute their products, and of the resources used to make them.

At organisational level an EMS would cover issues like:

- greenhouse gas (GHG) emissions
- energy use

- water use and wastage
- chemical use
- resource use
- business travel
- transport and distribution.

For manufacturing, the EMS would cover things like:

- proofing
- prepress
- printing
- inks
- energy use
- chemical use
- raw materials use.

In practical terms, for a printer committed to an environmental policy of reducing, re-using and recycling, this would involve initiatives on several fronts:

- the reduction of VOC emissions by:
    - o  using vegetable-based inks instead of mineral-based ones
    - o  printing using waterless litho
    - o  eliminating the use of acetone, IPA, or white spirit as a thinner for inks, or to clean surfaces
- the reduction of waste by:
    - o  re-using raw materials and resources wherever possible – for example, recycled paper
- recycling whatever cannot be re-used – for example, printing plates, waste paper, wrappings, cardboard and wood from palettes and packing cases.

When publishers combine their efforts with printers' efforts to be environmentally friendly, or socially responsible, the greatest gains can be made.

For publishers, this would entail:

- reducing initial print runs, and printing little and often in answer to demand
    - o  this virtually eliminates the risk of being left with unsold stock which, more often than not, ends up in landfill
- asking printers to use recycled instead of virgin paper
    - o  this reduces the demand for fresh trees to be felled, and all the effort and energy needed to convert them into virgin paper

- using distributed printing

  o    printing near the major markets reduces book miles, as well as costs, since books no longer need to travel half way round the world to reach their markets. For example, copies of a title with an Asian and a US market could be printed in the Far East as well as in the USA, and distributed from there.

Becoming environmentally aware and doing environmentally friendly things is a gradual process, and it doesn't happen overnight. You don't have to do everything at once, and not all your products necessarily lend themselves to being printed on recycled paper, in small quantities, in far-flung corners of the globe. Starting with a few titles and going from there is a good start; and, at least, it is a step in the right direction.

# 7 Binding and finishing

We have now come to the point when all the component parts of the book are going to be brought together to make up a single unit – the book. Binding and finishing are about to begin.

You and the editor have checked and approved the printing of the text, any separately printed illustrations and the jacket (or the cover); the binder's brasses have been made, the colour of the cloth for the case has been chosen and production orders have been issued.

Although the term binding is loosely used to mean everything that is done to printed sheets to turn them into a book, strictly speaking, it really only means joining folded sections together and putting them into some form of cover; while operations such as cutting, trimming, inserting, rounding and backing, casing-in, packing, etc., are part of finishing. In this chapter, I will use the word binding to cover everything.

## Where do you go for binding?

There are two choices. The first, and probably the more common, is to use a printer who has a bindery as part of their factory, and is able to offer you an all-in service. The second is to use a trade binder, whose sole function is to provide a binding service.

The advantages of using a printer-binder are that:

- the entire job is carried out under one roof, and you only need to deal with one supplier
- the uninterrupted workflow makes it easier for you to manage scheduling and quality, and to control them when things go wrong
- it is more efficient
- risk is limited.

The main disadvantage is that this option can be more expensive than using a trade binder, mainly because the printer-binder provides a wider range of services than the trade binder, and partly because the printer-binder's workflow is less flexible than the trade binder's, with the need to maintain the balance between work coming off the printing presses and going through the bindery.

Trade binding prices are generally lower than those you will get from a printer-binder, but the printer-binder option may well prove to be the more attractive when you take into account the extra work it takes to place a job with a trade binder, and which can involve:

- getting an estimate for the job
- scheduling the job, and ensuring that stock is printed and ready for dispatch to the trade binder by the due date
- organising and paying for transport of printed stock to the trade binder
- dealing with printing quality issues that may have an effect on the binding.

Obviously, trade binders do have their uses, as they are still in business. But it makes sense to consider all the aspects of both options, and not just the bottom line.

## Which binding method?

There is a wide range of methods to choose from, starting with:

- stapling
- ring binding
- spiral binding
- wire-O
- side stapling (also known as side-stitching, or side-stabbing)
- thermal binding
- comb binding
- post binding
- singer sewn binding.

Although these methods are most commonly used for leaflets, pamphlets, annual reports, dissertations, manuals, course notes, etc., they can be used for binding books as well.

More usually, though, when it comes to books, or what is known as *edition binding*, the range is limited to four methods:

- perfect binding
- notch, slotted, or burst binding
- section sewn binding
- saddle stitching.

The first three methods can be used for paperback (or limp) binding or hard-back (or cased) binding. What affects their choice is a combination of factors that have as much to do with marketing and perception of value for money, as they do with physical aspects of the book, and how well it functions. Because saddle-stitching has its own special uses I will deal with it last.

The first two methods are adhesive bindings, and their durability and strength depend on the quality of the glue, the ability of the paper to absorb and bond with the glue, and the weight of the book.

Modern adhesives, such as PUR adhesives, are generally available (though you should check with your binder that they use PUR adhesives, since not every binder is equipped to do so), which have virtually eliminated the problems associated with the older adhesives which used to vitrify and crack with age and use.

However, if you are planning to produce a perfect bound book which contains either a combination of coated and non-coated papers – for example, in a biography with separate sections of illustrations (plates) printed on coated paper – or is printed entirely on coated paper, you will find it useful to discuss your plans with the binder first. The weakest part of any adhesive-bound book is where two different types of paper meet, and if anywhere is going to fail, it will be here.

This is because coated papers are, by their nature, less absorbent than uncoated papers, and since the success of perfect binding depends on the degree to which paper absorbs and bonds with the adhesive, even PUR adhesives, you need to make certain that your book does not end up coming apart, once it is in the hands of the end-user.

Whereas perfect and notch binding depend for their strength on the interaction between paper and adhesives, section sewing depends for its strength on the action of the threads in locking the sections together in a vertical and horizontal grid. It is highly durable, but relatively expensive.

### Perfect binding

The cheapest binding method is perfect binding. This is most often used for paperback books, but can also be used for hardbacks. Most paperback printer-binders are able to produce perfect bound books. But some printer-binders may not be able to do so, choosing to produce notch bound books instead. So, it is important to find out if the supplier is able to handle the job.

The chief characteristic of perfect binding is that the spine fold of the folded sections is removed (as we will see later), which results in a book block made up of individual leaves of paper.

For example, a book of 160 pages printed as $10 \times 16$-page sections, will end up as a book block of 80 leaves.

Because there are no sections there are no spine folds, and this makes it easy to identify a perfect bound book.

The leaves are first glued together along their spine, and then glued directly to the spine of the cover. In hardback perfect binding, the book block is attached to the case by the lining and the endpapers.

The main defect with perfect binding is when leaves work loose from the glue, and come out of the book. However, with modern adhesives this defect is now quite rare.

Perfect binding is the most widely used binding method for paperbacks, and it is generally linked in the buyer's perception to cheapness and value for money. However, when it comes to perfect bound hardbacks, the opposite is almost true, with the market seeing perfect binding as a low quality option in producing something that is frequently associated with high quality, particularly if a perfect bound hardback costs the same as an equivalent sewn hardback.

Ironically, the increased numbers of perfect bound hardbacks coming from digital (print on demand) printers, where notch or sewn binding are not normally possible, is changing this perception: here, the market is primarily interested in having that content. How much it costs and how it is packaged are of secondary importance.

### Notch, slotted or burst binding

These three terms can be used interchangeably, though burst binding, strictly, refers to work produced on a web press.

This type of binding is not much more expensive than perfect binding, and is being increasingly used as an alternative to perfect binding, and as a substitute for section sewn binding, particularly for hardbacks.

Unlike in perfect binding, the section spine folds are not removed. So, a notch-bound 160-page book, printed as $10 \times 16$-page sections, will still be made up of ten sections when it is bound. The result is a strong, durable product where the pages do not fall out.

A series of notches or slots are cut along the length of the spine fold of each section in the book block. Glue is applied to the spine of the book block, which is then attached to spine of the cover, if the book is a paperback. In the case of a hardback, the book block is attached to the case by lining and the endpapers.

Notch-bound books and section-sewn books both have spine folds, so distinguishing one from the other can be difficult merely by looking at the outside of the book. You need to open the book, and go to the centre of a section. If you can see the thread from the section sewing, the book is likely to be section sewn, though there is always the possibility that it has been thread sealed. If you cannot see any thread, then the book is notch bound.

As mentioned above, section sewing is the most expensive binding method, but it is also the strongest and most durable, and can be used in paperback binding as well as hardback.

To give you an idea of the difference in cost between the different binding methods, look at the Table 7.1 which shows the difference in cost between perfect, notch and sewn binding, with perfect binding starting at a base of 100:

*Table 7.1* Cost of binding

| | |
|---|---|
| Perfect binding | 100 |
| Notch binding | 106 |
| Section sewn binding | 141 |

The strength in section-sewn binding comes from the fact that the book block is made up of sections, and not just leaves, and because each section is sewn vertically up its spine fold, and then joined to the neighbouring section by being horizontally sewn across the width of the book block, holding it tight in two directions.

### Saddle-stitching (also known as wire-stitching)

The last method used for edition binding is saddle-stitching, in which two wire staples are inserted through the spine of each section, and closed to hold the sections in the book together. You are most probably familiar with this method from seeing school exercise books, or from pamphlets.

Saddle-stitching is not terribly strong or durable, but it certainly has a place in edition binding, and that is when the extent is very short – say between 8 and 64 pages – and the paper is not bulky enough to allow for a spine.

Saddle-stitched books are constructed differently from perfect, notch or section-sewn books. Where these are (only initially in the case of a perfect-bound book) made up of sections gathered together side by side with each other to form a book block, saddle-stitched books are made up of sections which are inserted, or nested, inside each other, and then secured with two staples inserted into the spine fold and closed.

For example, in a 32-page saddle-stitched book, printed 4 pages to view, there are 4 × 8-page sheets:

- sheet 1 contains pages 1–4 and 29–32
- sheet 2 contains pages 5–8 and 25–28
- sheet 3 contains pages 9–12 and 21–24
- sheet 4 contains pages 13–16 and 17–20

Once the sheets have been folded, sheet 2 is inserted into sheet 1, sheet 3 into sheet 2, and sheet 4 into sheet 3. If there is a cover it will be wrapped round the inserted sheets, and everything is joined together and held in place with the two staples through the centre of the spine fold, and trimmed.

Saddle-stitched books are found in all shapes and sizes from poetry books to catalogues to guides to school exercise books – anywhere where a spine is not possible or not critical. The main problems with saddle-stitched work is that it is generally not very durable, and there is an upper limit to the extent which is about 112 pages, though obviously this depends on the bulk of the book. Plain paper covers are likely to work loose from the book and fall off, leaving little traces of paper caught in the staples. But even with thick laminated card covers this can happen too, over time and with use; and, with prolonged exposure to damp conditions, staples rust and corrode, causing the paper inside the book to stain, and the cover to work loose and drop off.

## Binding and finishing

Binding (for short) is made up of a series of processes whose purpose is to assemble and join together all the different pieces that go to make up a book.

This may be as simple as a few pages stapled into a paper cover, or as complex as a hardback book, with a printed, laminated paper case, separate plate sections, head and tail bands, register ribbon and laminated jacket.

Each process takes the output from the preceding process and transforms it into an output for the process that follows. Some of these processes are linear – for example, folding, gathering and binding. While others, like case making, cover printing or laminating, produce components that are timed to join the workflow at specific points, which depend on how the supplier organises it. For example, a supplier producing perfect bound paperbacks on an in-line binding machine needs all the components there at the start of the job.

The processes start out pretty much the same, but start to diverge, according to the binding style and product, once the book block has been gathered together.

## Folding

If you have printed your sheets on a web press, they will be delivered as folded sections. So, your folding has already been done for you, and you can skip this stage. It is worth remembering, if you are producing a lot of books, that this, and the high speeds at which web presses run, can yield distinct advantages in terms of time, and to a certain extent, the money saved.

If your job has been printed on a sheet-fed press, the sheets need to be folded into sections (also known as signatures). If your sheets have been printed on a very large sheet to get the most out of the size of the printing press, the sheet will need to be slit in half, before it can fit onto the binder's folding machines (folders). You may also find it necessary to slit the sheet, especially if the paper is bulky. This is because bulky papers are difficult to fold in 32s, and crease at the top and along the head of the section. Folding in 16s eliminates the problem. If the job is being done by a printer-binder there is no need to tell the binder about this. But, if you are using a trade binder, you will need to make sure they know.

Folding is done according to an imposition scheme, which ensures that, if the sheet is correctly folded, the pages in that section will run in the correct sequence, and appear the right way up, with the correct margins. There are a large number of impositions, each one of which is designed for a specific purpose. Bearing in mind that it is possible to fold a 16-page section in as many as eight different ways, it is absolutely essential, if you are using a trade binder, for the printer and binder to agree on the imposition scheme, before the job is printed. Usually it is the binder who specifies the imposition, as it is their folders that have to deal with the printed sheets – all the printer has to do is put ink on paper. Saddle-stitched work has a different set of imposition schemes.

For notch binding, the notches are cut into the spine during folding. On a web press this is done before the folded sections are delivered at the end of the printing process. For sheet-fed work it is done on the binder's folder.

### Gathering

Sheets are folded into sections. A 160-page book, printed in 32-page sections, will contain five sections, each identified by a letter of the alphabet, though some are now numbered. The first section is Section A (pp. 1–32), the second section is Section B (pp. 33–64), and so on to the last section, Section E (pp. 129–60). For a run of 1,000 copies of this book, there are now five piles of sections, each one containing 1,000 copies of each section, which need to be gathered together to become the book block.

This is done in a process known as gathering, in which one copy of each section is combined to form the book block.

Before the book block is bound (after which putting mistakes right can be either expensive, very expensive or impossible, depending on the binding method), each book block is checked to make sure that:

- it contains the right number of sections (none missing, and non duplicated)
- each section is the right way up
- each section has been folded correctly, and is in the right sequence.

This process, known as collating, is done visually (by a person or by a magic eye if the collating is done on an in-line binder) and involves looking at the collating mark (a small black rectangle) which has been printed to appear on the outside of the section on the spine fold. If the book block has been correctly gathered, the collating marks march diagonally down the spine from the head to the tail. Any mistakes, such as those described above, will interrupt the progress of the line, and show which section is at fault.

## Binding

The book block is now ready to be joined together.

### Perfect binding: paperback

If your book is going to be perfect bound, the book block has to lose its spine folds. This is done by passing the book block over a milling wheel which grinds off the spine folds, to leave a rough and nicely absorbent surface ready for the adhesive, which is used to hold the leaves together, and to attach the cover to the spine. As described in Chapter 5 on raw materials, there are lots of adhesives to choose from, each one with a set of properties which make them more or less suitable for a given job, which makes it essential to discuss your requirements with the supplier to make sure you get the best.

Before it is fed into the binding line, the outside of the cover is scored on either side of the spine to make sure that it folds neatly round the book block without creasing. For greater strength, some publishers ask for an extra line to be scored onto the front and back board about 3mm out from the spine to create a hinge, which is then glued to the first and last pages of the book.

Once the glue has dried enough to allow it, the book and its cover are trimmed along the top-, fore- and tail-edges, using a three-knife trim, and packed ready for dispatch. Perfect-bound paperbacks are flat (or square) backed.

### Perfect binding: hardback

The book block for perfect-bound hardback binding has a set of endpapers attached to the outer leaf of the first and last sections, about three millimetres from edge of the spine fold, so that they escape the milling process when the spine folds are removed. The milled spine is coated with glue, and a single flexible lining (made of crepe paper or calico cloth) is attached to the spine, with about five millimetres passing round the front and back of the book to be used for attaching the book block to the case.

The book block is then trimmed on three sides, and forwarded for casing-in, for which see below.

### Notch binding: paperback

In notch binding the spine folds are kept intact. The cover is glued to the spine of the book block which, when dry enough, is trimmed on three sides, and packed. Notch-bound paperbacks are flat backed.

### Notch binding: hardback

This is virtually the same process as for perfect-bound hardback binding, the only difference being that the spine folds are not milled off, which means that the endpapers, attached to the first and last pages of the first and last sections, can come right up to the edges of the section.

### Section sewn: paperback

Each section in the book block is sewn vertically along its spine fold; and all the sections are then joined together by being sewn horizontally across the book block. Before the cover is glued to the spine, the book is nipped to reduce any tendency to swelling at the spine caused by the sewing. After this, the cover is glued to the spine of the book block, trimmed on three sides, and packed. Sewn paperbacks are flat backed.

### Section sewn: hardback

The book block is sewn in exactly the same way as a sewn paperback, and endpapers are attached. When this has been completed, the book block needs to be prepared for casing-in. The first step is to nip the book block to expel any excess air and to reduce any swelling at the spine, caused by sewing. The spine is given a coating of glue, and the book block is then trimmed on three sides. If the book is to be flat backed, the next two processes are omitted. However, if you want a book with a rounded spine, the book block needs to rounded and backed – backing (or jointing) produces the shoulder on either side of the spine. Finally, the spine is reinforced with a mull (cloth) or linen lining, though more frequently this is now stretchable crepe paper, called flexilining. For extra strength a second lining may be added, but for most edition binding a single lining is considered to be enough.

The book block is now ready for casing-in.

### Casing-in

In this process, the book block is attached to the case by applying glue to the endpapers and pressing them onto the boards of the binding case. The cased-in book passes through a series of clamps and presses, which give it its shape: either as a flat-backed or as a rounded and backed book. Many books are cased-in so that when the book is open there is a hollow between the spine of the case and the spine of the book block. This kind of style is known as hollow back (or open back) binding. The opposite of this is tight back binding, where the spine of the book block is glued to the spine of the case. Tight back binding is useful for particularly heavy books, where there is a danger of the book tearing itself out of the case. However, frequent use can cause the foil used in blocking and any decoration on the spine to flex and crack.

With casing-in completed, the book is ready to be jacketed and packed, ready for dispatch.

## Components: covers, printed paper cases, jackets, plate sections, printed endpapers

Covers, jackets, plate sections and printed endpapers need to be available before binding starts. If the complete job is being produced under one roof by a printer-binder, there is little you need do, apart from specifying what you want, and checking that it is what you asked for.

Making sure that components are printed in time is the supplier's responsibility not yours.

If you are organising the components instead, you must make sure that work starts on them so that they can be delivered to the binder in time for stock to acclimatise to the atmospheric conditions in the bindery.

We have already looked at the raw materials that go into making a book, let's look now at how they are used in real life, so to speak.

### Paperback covers

Paperbacks are bound in board, also called cover card, which weighs anywhere between 220 and 280gsm (the average weight is 240gsm). Cover card can be coated on both sides (double-sided), or on the printing surface only (single-sided), which costs less. It can also be uncoated. Coated cover card tends to be white for use in colour printing; but it is also available in an enormous range of shades.

When choosing cover card be sure to choose one whose grain, when bound, runs parallel with the spine (long grain) of the book. Paperbacks with long-grain covers open easily, and stay flat when open. Cross-grain covers crease and wrinkle as they are being glued to the spine; and they bow if the book is left flat.

While some covers are left uncoated for aesthetic reasons, the majority of covers are coated either using varnish (NC, UV or machine) or film lamination to protect them from scuffing and fingermarks, and to stop ink transferring to the reader's fingers.

### Hardback printed paper cases (PPCs), case wrap or cover to board

It is quite common to cover the case of a hardback in printed paper instead of in cloth (real or imitation). This style of binding is known variously as printed paper case (PPC), case wrap or cover to board. Books bound this way are often jacketed as well.

The paper used for printed paper cases is usually a single-sided 125gsm art paper – art paper, so that it can do justice to the colours, and single-sided so that it can absorb the glue used to attach it to the case. PPCs are either varnished or laminated.

As with covers, make sure you choose a long-grain paper, so that the grain runs parallel with the spine. Cross-grain papers will crease during gluing.

### Jackets

Most hardback books are jacketed. This is done to protect the case. But a jacket, like the cover on a paperback, can also be a powerful marketing tool, designed for impact, and to attract the attention of the potential buyer in the bookshop, or on the internet.

Jackets need to be reasonably tough to withstand repeated handling. If you are printing in colour, then you should go for a coated paper, which will allow the colours to appear at their best, starting at 125gsm. Unless you are printing on both sides of the jacket (unlikely), single-sided art paper is preferable to double-sided: it is cheaper, but more importantly it doesn't slide off the book, which happens with jackets printed on double-sided art paper. Make sure that the paper you choose has a grain that will end up running parallel with the book's spine

To protect the colours on the jacket, to stop them transferring to fingers and hands, and to give the jacket extra strength, it is usually laminated using a thin (12 micron) oriented polypropylene (OPP) film lamination, which is standard for jackets and covers.

Having said all this, it is worth remembering that some jackets are equally as attractive, especially in a book shop awash with a kaleidoscope of coloured jackets and covers, if they are printed in a single colour on a thick cartridge, and left unlaminated, on the principle that less is more.

*Plate (illustration) sections and tips*

Although it is quite common for books to be integrated, that is where the illustrations are printed together on the same page as the text, books still appear where the illustrations have been printed on a different paper, usually an art paper, and bound into the book in separate sections. This is usually the case where the ratio of pictures to text is low, and it makes more sense economically, and in terms of production, to print the text on, say, a book wove, and the illustrations on a 100–110gsm high-white long-grain art paper.

Folded sections can either be inserted into the middle of a text section, when they are known as an insert, or wrapped round the section, and called a wrap. Inserts and wraps should appear spaced regularly throughout the book, and should start at least two sections away from the start and end of the book, as much for appearance as for strength.

A single page of illustrations, such as a frontispiece appearing opposite a title page, is known as a tip, which is either glued to the outside of a section (a tip on) or in the middle of a section (tip in). Tipping in or on usually involves hand work, and since it is not part of the binding workflow, it becomes expensive in terms of time and money, and for this reason is best avoided.

*Endpapers*

While the main purpose of endpapers is to secure the book block to the case, they can also be printed for decoration, or to carry information, such as a map.

Endpapers, printed or plain, should be strong enough to support the weight of the book, and are usually made of strengthened cartridge paper, starting at 135gsm.

Where endpapers are plain and not printed, the binder will provide them, working to your specification for colour, weight and finish. When choosing an endpaper, make sure that its grain runs parallel with the book spine. This is important to prevent warping of the case.

If the endpapers are to be printed, you need to specify how: single-sided, double-sided, single-colour (PMS, with the PMS number) or 4-colour. If the binding is being done by a printer-binder all you need do is provide artwork (most usually in the form of a PDF file) and they will print them for you. But if you are binding at a trade bindery you may need to organise the printing elsewhere, and ensure that endpapers arrive at the bindery to meet the schedule.

If you are printing endpapers with the same image back and front, then which goes where is not a problem. Where endpapers differ, though, you need to let the binder know which one goes at the front and which at the back.

Sometimes books are cased-in using the first and last pages of the book block as endpapers. This is known as self-ending. It is cheaper than using endpapers, and uses otherwise unused pages in the book block. If the book is relatively short and not very heavy, then self-ending is a possibility, though there are marketing factors that need to be considered. You also need to take into account that the paper attaching the case to the book block has not been strengthened in the way that endpaper paper has been, and is two thirds of its weight (90gsm compared with 135gsm).

### Hardback cases

The cases for hardback books are made from a combination of board and covering – cloth (imitation or real), leather or plastic, glued together. The parts of the case are:

- front board
- spine
- back board.

Almost all cases used in edition binding are made using imitation cloth, with various finishes ranging from smooth to embossed, and in an enormous range of colours which you choose from a swatch that the binder should let you have.

Most cases are generally covered in one kind of material only, in which case they are full bound, or wholebound. However, it is possible to vary the look of the case by combining different materials (generally paper) in different proportions to produce cases which are:

- quarter bound – spine only in a different material
- half bound – spine and corners on front and back boards in a different material
- three-quarter bound – same as half bound but more so.

When specifying board weight, remember to match the thickness and weight to the format of the book. As a rule: the bigger the format, the heavier and thicker the boards.

### Blocking

To identify the book inside its case, the title and author's name are put on the spine. This is done by blocking, a process in which the lettering is stamped in metallic foil – gold, silver (both usually imitation) or any metallic shade – onto the spine using a die (sometimes called a chemac, which is a trade name, or a brass, which is what it was once, but is no longer, made of).

The binder normally arranges for the die to be made, but you need to let the binder have the artwork: lettering and any decoration you want to appear on the spine.

Sometimes the front board is blocked as well as the spine.

Blocking without using a foil is called blind blocking, and all you can see is the impression in the board made by the action of the die. Blind blocking is obviously very subtle. But can look good.

For extra decoration you can have a crusher panel, which is a rectangle of colour blocked onto the spine/front board, and onto which the lettering is then blocked.

For special, non-edition binding, such as a presentation copy, blocking and hand-tooling can really enhance the look of the book, especially if done in materials like leather or crash canvas.

### Head and tail bands

The head band is a piece of cord that is added to the head of the book block after it has been rounded and backed. If you have a head band, it is usual to have a tail band at the bottom of the book block as well. There are lots of designs and colours to choose from, and you will be able to make your choice from a swatch that the binder should let you have.

### Edge decoration

You can decorate the edges (head, fore and tail edges) either by gilding them, marbling or staining, in descending order of expense. This is done after the book block has been trimmed.

### Register ribbon, or ribbon marker

The register ribbon allows the reader to mark their place in the book. The ribbon is attached to the book block at the top of the spine before the head band is attached, and before casing in. The ribbon can be made from silk, cotton or any other fabric – natural or synthetic – and can provide a colourful and useful embellishment to the book. The colour and the type of material can be chosen from a swatch provided by the supplier.

### The oddment

An oddment is a section that has fewer pages in it than the other sections in the book, and it exists because the extent of your book does not make a section. For example, a book of 160 pages has ten 16-page sections, so there is no oddment. However, if the book is 168 pages long, and still printed in 16-page sections, there is an 8-page oddment. Obviously, it is best to try and avoid having an oddment. But if there is one, then in section sewn work, it is usual practice to position it at the back of the book, as the last signature but one, to give it protection from the stresses and strains of being a small section.

If the oddment has blank pages in (for example, if the last printed page is 164 there will be four blank pages), these will have to be carried over to the last section, to avoid blanks appearing in the middle of the text.

In perfect bound work, it is usual to put the oddment at the back of the book as the last section. If there are blanks you can either leave them in, or, as some do, cut them away – which is more expensive.

### Checking quality – lithographically printed books

Throughout the production process there have been opportunities for the supplier, and you, to check the quality of what is being produced. For the supplier, quality is being constantly checked during each process. For you, quality checks usually come at the end of a process, before the output from that process becomes the input for the next. So, for example, immediately after printing, you will receive a folded and trimmed set of printed sheets (running sheets), so that you can check:

- printing quality
- that the imposition has produced pages that run in the correct sequence
- that margins are correctly spaced.

Once you have approved these running sheets, binding can start.

If, however, you find problems in the running sheets, now is the time to put things right: it is quicker, easier and cheaper to reprint a section than having to replace a faulty page in a bound book. This can be a major operation for section sewn books, and is virtually impossible for perfect bound books – the only option, there, being to pulp the entire print run and start again!

The next time you check quality is when you see an advance copy, taken from bulk stock, before it is packed and delivered to your warehouse.

For all books, you should check that:

- the book block has been bound in the right way up
- pages appear in the right sequence
- running heads are evenly aligned, and do not move up and down
- margins are correct throughout the book (the back margin is usually the narrowest)
- the edges have been clean trimmed, and do not show nicks from the guillotine blade.

For perfect- and notch-bound paperbacks you need to check that:

- the strength of the binding, especially if the book contains two different types of paper, or if the book has been printed on a heavy art paper
- the book block has been trimmed square
- the cover has been drawn on square, and has not creased during gluing
- glue from the spine has not seeped onto the front and last pages of the book block, or onto the head and tail edges of the spine
- the hinge (if you have asked for one) on the front and back panels is properly stuck to the first and last pages of the book block, and that glue does not seep out from under the hinge.

You should also check how flexible the book feels, how easily it opens, whether it lies flat when opened and left on a table, and how long it remains open at the same page.

For section-sewn paperbacks, the checking process is much the same as for a perfect-bound paperback. However, the strength of the binding comes from the fact that it is sewn, and not glued. Because it is sewn, you need to make certain that the book is not wedge shaped, which will happen if the spine with its extra bulk coming from the threads is not properly nipped before the cover is attached. It is also important to check that glue has not seeped into the spine gutter through the thread holes. This is particularly important if the book has plate sections in it printed on art paper, as the glue can pick off the coating, and cause white patches (hickeys) to appear at the spine.

For section-sewn hardbacks, checking the book block is the same as for a sewn paperback. Your attention is really focused on the case, the endpapers and any other embellishments, such as head and tail bands, or coloured edges that you may have added.

Checking the case involves make sure that:

- the covering has been smoothly attached to the boards, that there are no lumps underneath, and that the length of the turned over edges of the covering is consistent right round the front and back boards, and is neatly trimmed
- the case is square
- the endpapers are pasted in square, there are no lumps underneath, and that the lining has been properly attached to the first and last pages of the book block
- the back lining runs parallel with the spine all the way down the case, is neatly trimmed, and is not excessive
- the corners of the covering have been neatly mitred, and do not rise underneath the endpapers
- the blocking is square (especially if you have asked for a crusher panel), and the foil is not peeling
- the boards are not warping or bowing.

The quality of the casing-in needs to be checked, and, if the book is rounded and backed, you should see how well the spine and the fore edge of the book block keep their shape (the spine should be convex, and the fore edge should be concave). You should also check that the case overlaps the edges of the book block consistently all round by 3–4mm, which is standard.

If you want to test the strength of the casing-in, open the book up, and hold it by its boards only, with the book block dangling by its endpapers (so to speak). If it stays in its case without pulling away from the boards, and regains its shape when closed, you can be sure that the casing-in has been well done.

Finally, if you have asked for them, check that:

- the head and tail bands are properly attached
- the register ribbon is also properly attached
- the stain on stained edges has not feathered into the pages.

*Binding digitally produced books*

Digitally produced books are bound differently from books printed lithographically. Where these are produced in relatively large quantities in 16s or 32s, a digitally printed book is treated as a single unit, each one of which is printed one at a time page by page (or leaf by leaf), perfect bound, covered and trimmed in line, before the next book is started. There are no sheets to fold, sections to gather and collate, no spine fold to grind off.

A book produced digitally can be packed and ready for dispatch within a few hours of being ordered. Since this leaves no room for you to check quality, the responsibility (and associated risk) for doing this passes to the supplier. Given the numbers of single copy orders they fulfil each day, it goes without saying that their quality management systems throughout the process are extremely well developed, as mistakes have to be rare indeed.

This brings us to the end of the chapter on binding. The next step in getting your books to market is to pack them and arrange for their transport from the bindery to a warehouse if you intend to store them there; or for their dispatch directly to customers.

## Binding and the environment

Binding, when compared with certain types of printing, is relatively pollution free. When it comes to waste, almost all binders now operate a waste management scheme where post-consumer waste – trimmings, rejects, spoiled sheets, spoiled covers and jackets – is collected from the shop floor and sent off for recycling.

# 8 Getting stock into the warehouse; and legal matters

Once you have approved the advanced bound copies, you are now ready to issue instructions for stock to be packed and dispatched. Books can be dispatched either as single copies direct to the customer, which is usually the case with print-on-demand jobs, or they can be moved in bulk from the printer to a central point, which could be either the publisher's warehouse, a wholesaler or a book supply service.

Although practice varies from publisher to publisher, generally speaking, your involvement with, and responsibility for, the project ends when stock has been successfully delivered to the warehouse and signed for.

## Packing and dispatch: single copy, or small quantity, orders

For single copy or small orders, it is usual for the printer to provide a same-day packing and dispatch service, which involves everything from shrink wrapping the book and packing it in a protective padded envelope (known as a *Jiffy bag*), or a carton, to addressing it, and arranging for it to be sent off as quickly as possible to the customer, which could just as easily be a publisher, a wholesaler, a retailer or a private individual.

For orders which involve heavy or highly priced books, it is worth considering a sturdier form of packing to provide extra protection. This could either be a thick cardboard sleeve, which can be sealed at either end; or, for greater protection, a thick cardboard carton inside a cardboard outer sleeve, which has been specially made to match the book's weight and dimensions. For this, you will need to discuss the specification with the supplier.

## Packing stock: bulk orders

For longer print runs, stock is usually delivered to a warehouse, from where it is dispatched in various quantities in response to orders coming in from wholesalers and retailers.

Packing stock and arranging for it to be delivered to the warehouse is done by the supplier, in response to instructions issued by you, most usually as part of the binding order.

Before books are packed into cartons or parcels, they can be shrink wrapped individually. Doing this certainly protects the book from being damaged or soiled in the book shop, but it may also act as a disincentive to the prospective buyer, who may not feel like breaking open the wrapping.

Multiple copies, or sets, of a book can be packed in several ways:

- shrink wrapping
- in cardboard boxes, or cartons
- in binder's parcels, which are made of strong brown (kraft) paper, rather like the paper used for carrying groceries and shopping in.

Whichever way is chosen, it is conventional to limit the weight of each package to around 13–13.5kg, mainly because this weight is relatively easy to handle, and it puts less strain on the packing materials. This is especially true of binder's parcels and cardboard boxes, which have a tendency to split if overloaded, spilling out and damaging books in the process.

Each package should carry a label stuck on at each end, so that it doesn't matter which end faces out in the warehouse, carrying the following information:

- author name
- book title
- edition (first, second, thumb index, etc.)
- impression (first, second, etc.)
- number of copies in the package
- binding style (needed for hardback or paperback; or special style: leather with register ribbon)
- international standard book number (ISBN)
- bar code
- name of supplier.

The packets of books are then stacked onto a pallet, or skid (a wooden, plastic or metal platform, which can be lifted and moved by fork lift truck), and then either shrink wrapped, or strapped, to prevent the load from shifting during transit. Shrink wrapping is much gentler on stock than strapping, which is sturdier, but can cause damage to stock unless it is protected by an interface material like wood or cardboard to allow the straps to dig in and prevent movement.

Although, pallet weight and height must ultimately depend on the requirements of individual warehouses, the optimum weight of the loaded pallet should not be more than 1000 kilos, or one tonne; and the optimum height should not be more than 180cms/1.8 metres.

These limits ensure that the pallet can be:

- moved around by fork lift truck
- supported by warehouse shelving or racking
- fitted into warehouse racking.

Pallets come in six sizes which conform to ISO Standard 6780. The sizes are:

*Table 8.1* Pallet sizes

| Dimensions (width × length) | Area most used |
| --- | --- |
| 1219 × 1016mm | North America |
| 1000 × 1200mm | Europe and Asia |
| 1165 × 1165mm | Australia |
| 1067 × 1067mm | North America, Europe, Asia |
| 1100 × 1100mm | Asia |
| 800 × 1200mm | Europe |

Choice of size depends on where the pallet is most used, and where it is being transported to. Most British publishers specify either of the two Euro-pallets – 1000 × 1200mm and 800 × 1200mm – the smaller size making it ideal if it has to go through narrow doorways. Pallets are either four-way entry, which means that they can be picked up from any side, or two-way entry, with the preference being for four-way entry pallets.

## Moving stock to the warehouse

How stock is moved from the supplier to the warehouse is going to depend on where stock is being produced. Stock produced in the UK and Europe is normally transported overland in a lorry (or truck); while stock produced in other parts of the world is most likely to come by sea, either in a container (especially if it is a large job, or it has been consolidated with other of your jobs) or as general cargo. It is possible to use air freight, but the costs are very high, and effectively make this a last ditch option. If you need copies that quickly, it would be worthwhile arranging a short-run job nearer home to fill the need until bulk stock arrives.

### How long does it take?

If your job has been produced in the UK, moving stock from the supplier to the warehouse is relatively simple, and delivery can normally be completed in one day. Stock coming in from Europe may take from between a week to ten days, though this obviously depends on distance as well as conditions on the roads, particularly during winter. For stock coming by sea, either from the Far East or the United States, it is usual to allow five to six weeks, which includes time at sea, customs clearance at each end and delivery to the destination warehouse.

### Arranging transport and organising documentation

Arranging transport and organising documentation is time consuming, and requires a good deal of specialised knowledge. So much so, that it is rarely done by people in production, and is more usual to use a supplier who is able to do this for you as part of their service. If the supplier is not able to do this for you, then it is worth using the services of a freight-forwarder, which would include everything from providing full documentation to arranging for stock to be picked up from the supplier, clearing customs formalities at both ends, and delivering stock to the warehouse at the final destination.

For sea freight, the documentation includes the following.

- Ocean bill of lading (BOL, B/L): this is a legal document issued by the shipper to the carrier. As such, it is a contract, and must contain details of the type, quantity and destination of the goods being carried, as well as the shipper's name, the carrier's name, the flag of nationality and registration of the vessel and the overall weight and dimensions of the load.
- Commercial invoice: all consignments need a commercial invoice, which provides details of what the goods are and their value.

Additionally, you may be asked to provide:

- a certificate of origin (CO), which certifies where the products were made, and may be required for political or commercial reasons
- an inspection certificate (IC), which certifies that the goods to be exported were inspected to establish that, before they leave the port of departure, they:
  - o   meet the original specifications
  - o   are in good condition
  - o   in the quantity asked for.

Stock coming in overland from the Continent, should be covered by the International Road Transport (TIR) convention, which allows goods being moved 'to, from and between other European, North African and near Asian countries ... to cross one or more international border with minimal customs involvement.'(HM Revenue and Customs website.) This is made possible by using a system of international documents, which allow goods to move through different countries without having to pay any duty until they arrive at their final destination. TIR has simplified a once complex process, and all the lorry driver needs is a consignment note (or inland bill of lading) listing what is contained in the load, and a commercial invoice giving the value of the goods.

## Communication

As with all project management, good communication is a key factor in achieving success, and never more so than at the end of the project, when time is short, and the risk of anything going wrong carries a high penalty – for example, stock not arriving in time to meet the publication date. Because publishers work in different ways and have different procedures, it is important for the supplier to know what these are, by being given clear instructions at the outset about what to do with stock in terms of packing and delivery. For example, some publishers ask suppliers, or forwarding agents, to arrange a specific day and time to deliver stock in order to avoid congestion at the warehouse; while for others, this may not be thought necessary.

Suppliers need to know if stock is destined for different parts of the globe as part of a dropped, or split, shipment, and how to identify that stock so that it reaches the right place, and the right customer. The same is true where there are different language versions of the stock, like in co-edition publishing.

Whatever the case, it is important to avoid things going wrong and it is best to adopt a belt and braces attitude, double checking everything, first to make sure that it has been properly specified, and second to be certain that the supplier/forwarding agent understands what they are being asked to do.

### *Insurance and risk*

Transporting stock around in ships, or lorries, by air or by rail, has its attendant risks. Books may be lost, stolen, damaged or delayed, all of which can have serious financial consequences for the publisher. So, it is essential to make sure that stock is properly insured before it leaves the supplier.

There is a wide variety of insurance options to choose from, ranging from simple insurance against loss and damage to insurance against:

- loss
- accidental damage
- damage during loading
- delay
- theft
- negligence.

The more risks you cover yourself against, the more expensive the insurance.

The International Chamber of Commerce has created a set of international commercial terms (or rules) which define the 'tasks, costs and risks associated with the transportation and delivery of goods'(ICC website).

International commercial terms (also known as *incoterms*) are three-letter acronyms; the ones you are most likely to meet are these.

- EXW (Ex works, from a named place of delivery): in an EXW transaction, the supplier makes stock available to the buyer at the supplier's premises, and is not responsible for anything else. The buyer is responsible for arranging and paying all the costs of:

    o   transport
    o   freight
    o   loading and unloading
    o   customs clearance

o   insurance
o   delivery to their own premises.

- FOB (free on board, in a named port of shipment): in an FOB arrangement, the supplier's responsibility ends when the goods have passed over the rail of a named ship at the port of shipment. From then on, the buyer is responsible for:

o   freight
o   unloading
o   customs clearance
o   insurance
o   delivery to their own premises.

- CIF (cost, insurance, freight, to a named port of destination): in a CIF deal, the supplier is responsible for paying the cost of insurance and freight up to the moment when the goods pass over the named ship's rail at the specified port of destination. At that point, risk in the goods passes to the buyer, who is responsible for all the costs involved in:

o   unloading
o   customs clearance
o   insurance
o   delivery to their own premises.

- DDP (delivery duty paid to a named place of destination): this is the deluxe arrangement, and the most expensive. It involves the supplier in the maximum risk and effort, and the buyer in virtually none. It is basically the opposite of EXW, and requires the supplier to arrange and pay for:

o   transport
o   freight
o   loading and unloading
o   customs clearance
o   insurance
o   delivery to the buyer's premises.

## Environmental issues

Moving books around the globe has an environmental impact: lorries, planes, ships and trains all have a greater or smaller carbon footprint, and most publishers are now aware of the fact that their products may have to travel quite long distances (known as book miles) before they reach their final destination in the hands of the reader.

Publishers who want to reduce their contribution to book miles have several options to choose from, the most radical of which is not to print books at all, and to convert to e- or online publishing. At one stroke this would eliminate book miles altogether. Failing this, publishers can choose to print locally. This doesn't necessarily mean that British publishers have to print in the UK. What it does mean is that printing can now be done as near as possible to where the major markets are for that product (another term for this is distributed printing). So, for example, if the major markets for a book are in the USA and Australia, then printing and distribution are done in these countries, avoiding the need to send stock half way round the world to reach them.

Another option is distributed distribution, which involves printing in one place, and distributing stock from there to the major markets, rather than bringing it all the way back to the publisher's warehouse, and distributing it from there. So, to take an example, a British publisher has 2,500 copies of a book printed in China. There are orders for 500 copies for Australia, and 500 for the USA. Rather than bringing stock back to the UK and then sending it from there to Australia and the USA, copies are sent directly from China. Doing this reduces the book miles, in this case, by some 42 per cent, from 21,700 miles to 12,500. This is certainly an option worth considering, and there are freight forwarders who are able to handle this kind of work.

## Contractual and legal issues

Just as there are contractual obligations and responsibilities for buyers (the publisher) and sellers (the supplier) during printing and binding, which are spelt out in the terms and conditions printed on the back of the supplier's estimate, so there are with the delivery of the goods and payment.

Suppliers base their conditions of contract on a set of standard terms prepared by the British Printing Industries Federation (BPIF), which makes it easier for all concerned, though suppliers may adapt the standard to suit their needs. The terms and conditions in the examples below are taken from a printer's terms and conditions.

The clauses of particular relevance to this part of the production cycle are concerned with delivery, risk and retention of title, payment, claims and liability. Most of them are pretty self-explanatory, but where necessary I have provided a comment to make sure their implications are clear.

### Variations in quantity

> Every endeavour will be made to deliver the correct quantity ordered, but estimates are conditional upon margins of five per cent for work in one colour only and 10 per cent for other work being allowed for overs or shortage (four per cent and eight per cent respectively for quantities exceeding 50,000) the same to be charged or deducted

**Comment:** this may not generally be a problem, particularly if you are dealing with low value books, where a shortfall of five per cent on a print run of 1,000 copies may not have much effect on the finances. However, if you are dealing with a high value book, a shortfall of one copy may be unacceptable. If this is the case, you should talk to the supplier before you place the work with them, and make sure they are aware of this.

*Delivery*

(a) Delivery of work shall be accepted when tendered and thereupon, or if earlier on notification that the work has been completed, payment shall become due.

(b) Unless otherwise agreed in writing completion and delivery times are a guide only and, whilst the seller will make every effort to adhere to proposed timescales, time is not of the essence in any contract with the buyer.

(c) Unless otherwise specified the price is for delivery of the work to the buyer's address as set out in the estimate. A charge may be made to cover any extra costs involved for delivery to a different address.

(d) Unless otherwise agreed in writing, (in which case an extra charge may be made) delivery will be to kerbside at the buyer's address and the buyer will make arrangements for off-loading and for any additional transportation to its storage facility.

(e) Subject to any agreement as per (d) above, delivery involving difficult access and/or unreasonable distance from vehicular access shall entitle the seller to make an extra charge to reflect its extra costs.

(f) Should expedited delivery be agreed the seller shall be entitled to make an extra charge to cover any overtime or any other additional costs.

**Comment:** Clause (a) is to make sure that goods are accepted at the warehouse when they are delivered and are not sent back to the supplier. To guard against this, make sure that the warehouse and the supplier have talked to each other and agreed delivery arrangements before stock leaves the supplier's premises, especially if it is going to leave earlier than originally scheduled. Sending stock back to the supplier because it was unexpected is expensive, may damage the relationship between buyer and supplier and could have a knock-on effect on the publication schedule.

Clause (b) is there to prevent the buyer from refusing to accept the goods, or asking for a discount if they have been completed late. This clause is related to the clause (d) under Liability, which states without equivocation: The seller shall not be liable for indirect loss, consequential loss or third party claims occasioned by delay in completing the work or for any loss to the buyer arising from delay in transit, whether as a result of the seller's negligence or otherwise.

Clause (c) covers what is known as a split delivery, which costs more than delivering to a single address. If you know there is going to be a split delivery, make sure this is clear in the specification so that any costs can be included in the estimate and do not appear later as extra costs. Extra costs at the end of the job are not a good thing, they have not been included in the estimating and pricing, and therefore eat away at the book's financial contribution to the company.

The same holds true for clause (f): if you know you need expedited delivery, try and include it in the specification.

Clauses (d) and (e) are self-explanatory. The only comment is that kerbside can be taken to mean to the warehouse entrance, rather than on the roadside. But delivery does mean delivery, and not off-loading, which should be done by the buyer's warehouse staff, not the lorry driver.

### Risk and retention of title

---

(a) The risk in all goods delivered in connection with the work shall pass to the buyer on delivery, and the buyer should insure accordingly.

(b) Goods supplied by the seller remain the seller's property until the buyer has paid for them and discharged all other debts owing to the seller.

(c) If the buyer becomes subject to insolvency, and the goods have not been paid for in full, the seller may take the goods back and, if necessary, enter the buyer's premises to do so, or to inspect and/or label the goods so as to identify them clearly.

(d) If the buyer shall sell the goods before they have been paid for in full they shall hold the proceeds of sale on trust for the seller in a separate account until any sum owing to the seller has been discharged from such proceeds.

---

**Comment:** Clauses (b) and (d) usually present no problem, even when the buyer starts selling the goods before they have paid for them, which is usually the case when the buyer and seller have come to an agreement over credit facilities. For example, on 1 June a printer delivers 1,000 copies of a book to a publisher, whose publication date is set for 28 June. The printer has agreed a 60-day credit period with the publisher, so payment falls due on 30 July. Between 28 June and 30 July, the publisher has been selling goods which still belong to the printer, and are effectively not theirs to sell. However, the printer by giving the publisher credit, has implicitly agreed to this. To some extent clause (d) protects the printer's financial interests. It is only in the case of the buyer becoming insolvent that the main purpose of clauses (b)–(d) becomes apparent, and that is to prevent the insolvency administrator from treating goods which have been delivered, but not paid for, as if they belonged to the buyer. This is why the printer reserves the right to enter the publisher's premises to label their property as theirs.

## *Payment*

> (a) Payment shall become due before delivery of the work. The seller, at their absolute discretion, may ask for part or full payment in advance of starting the work.
>
> (b) If credit facilities have been granted, payment is due by the end of the month following the month of invoice. If any item(s) remain unpaid by that due date charges will apply, in accordance with S5A and/or S6 of the Late Payment Commercial Debt (Interest) Act 1998 or any subsequent enactment. In addition, all invoices will become due and payable immediately and will be treated as overdue items, with appropriate charges applied and all costs reasonably incurred in collecting the debt payable by the buyer.
>
> (c) Unless otherwise agreed in writing, the price of the work will be 'ex-works' and delivery shall be charged extra.

**Comment:** in clause (a), the timing of payment is going to depend very much on what has been agreed between the two parties, and covers a wide range of options which vary according to the credit-worthiness of the buyer, and their relationship with the supplier. At one end of the scale a first-time customer may be required to pay for everything in full before the job starts, while at the other end, established customers others may be offered 60 days credit from the date of the invoice. Clause (c) is the default option, and you can override this by choosing any of the delivery terms described above, as long as they are made known to the supplier at the time of estimating.

## *Claims*

> (a) Advice of damage, delay or loss of goods in transit or of non-delivery must be given in writing to the seller and the carrier within three clear days of delivery (or, in the case of non-delivery, within three days of notification of despatch of the goods) and any claim in respect thereof must be made in writing to the seller and the carrier within seven clear days of delivery (or, in the case of non-delivery, within

seven days of notification of despatch). All other claims must be made in writing to the seller within 14 days of delivery. The seller shall not be liable in respect of any claim unless the aforementioned requirements have been complied with except in any particular case where the buyer proves that:

(i) it was not possible to comply with the requirements; and

(ii) the claim was made as soon as reasonably possible.

(b) If the work is defective so that the buyer may in law reject it, said rejection must take place within seven days of delivery of the goods, failing which the buyer will be deemed to have accepted the work.

(c) In the event of all or any claims or rejections the seller reserves the right to inspect the work within seven days of the claim or rejection being notified.

**Comment:** Clauses (a)–(c): given the relatively short time in which to make a claim, or to reject stock because it is defective, it is essential for warehouse staff to check stock as soon after delivery as possible to make sure that it has not been damaged, that it is all there, and that it is not defective. If stock is delayed, the warehouse should let the production department know so that they can take the matter up with the supplier. Production department responsibility for stock only ends when it has been accepted into the warehouse and signed for. It is worth bearing in mind that rejecting stock at this stage in the publishing cycle because it is defective is likely to have a serious impact on your publication date, and possibly the financial health and reputation of the company. The place to discover defective work is at advanced copy stage, not after stock has been delivered and stored in the warehouse.

*Liability*

(a) Insofar as is permitted by law where work is defective for any reason, including negligence, the seller's liability (if any) shall be limited to rectifying such defect, or crediting its value against any invoice raised in respect of the work.

(b) Where the seller performs their obligations to rectify defective work under this condition the seller shall not be liable for indirect loss, consequential loss or third party claims occasioned by defective work, and the buyer shall not be entitled to any further claim in respect of the work nor shall the buyer be entitled to repudiate the contract, refuse to pay for the work or cancel further deliveries.

(c) Defective work must be returned to the seller before replacement or credits can be issued. If the subject work is not available to the seller the seller will hold that the buyer has accepted the work and no credits or replacement work will be provided.

(d) The seller shall not be liable for indirect loss, consequential loss or third party claims occasioned by delay in completing the work or for any loss to the buyer arising from delay in transit, whether as a result of the seller's negligence or otherwise.

(e) Where the seller offers to replace defective work the buyer must accept such an offer unless they can show clear cause for refusing so to do. If the buyer opts to have the work re-done by any third party without reference to the seller the buyer automatically revokes their right to any remedy from the seller, including but not exclusively the right to a credit in respect of work done by the seller.

(f) Where the work will be forwarded by or on behalf of the buyer to a third party for further processing the buyer will be deemed to have inspected and approved the work prior to forwarding and the seller accepts no liability for claims arising subsequent to the third party's processing.

(g) The seller reserves the right to reject any work forwarded to them after initial processing by a third party as soon as is reasonably practicable without processing the work any further. Should the buyer require the seller notwithstanding to continue, then the seller is only obliged to do so after confirmation from the buyer in writing.

(h) Nothing in these conditions shall exclude the seller's liability for death or personal injury as a result of their negligence.

**Comment:** Clause (a) limits the supplier's liability to putting right any defective work. It does not include consequential loss, however that term may be interpreted.

Clause (b): if the supplier puts the defective work right, the matter ends there, and the buyer has no right to make any further claim, to refuse to pay for the work, or to cancel further deliveries of the job.

Clause (c): defective work must be returned to the supplier, so that they can put it right. Although not specifically stated, this should be at the supplier's expense, and under their insurance, as should be its return to the warehouse after rectification.

Clause (e): if the supplier offers to replace or make right defective work, and you refuse this offer, and send it to another supplier to put things right, you automatically forfeit the right to make any further claim against the original supplier, which is not a situation that the buyer would want to put themselves in, unless the original supplier is incapable of putting things right.

Clause (f): covers the situation where, for example, you are sending printed sheets to a trade binder to be bound and finished. You should check that sheets are alright before they leave the printer's premises, so that should defects be discovered, claims can be made to the right supplier.

Clause (g): covers the situation where, for example, a binder receives defective sheets from a printer. In this case, the binder will only start binding if they have received written permission from you to do so, on the understanding that they will not be held liable for a product that may turn out to be defective.

*Law*

---

These conditions and all other express and implied terms of the contract shall be governed and construed in accordance with the laws of England and Wales.

---

**Comment:** For work being carried out in England and Wales, this clause has force, because English law applies in the jurisdiction of England and Wales. However for work being carried out overseas, or even in Scotland, which has its own legal system, English law does not apply; which raises the interesting question of what happens when an English publisher wishes to go to court in pursuit of a legal remedy against a Chinese, or Spanish, supplier, for example; or vice versa.

It is important for companies to have written terms and conditions which show how they carry on their business; and it is important for these to be as standardised as possible to avoid the need for suppliers to have to negotiate a new set each time they start working with a new customer. The terms and conditions act as a framework within which business is carried out, and most suppliers and their customers operate comfortably and harmoniously within this framework, aware of their responsibilities and obligations. When things go wrong, both parties try as hard as possible to achieve a working compromise that satisfies both parties. As such, there is, in most cases, little need to have recourse to law; and this should really only become necessary when all other options have been tried and found not to work.

# Further reading

Generally speaking the publishing industry writes about itself relatively little, and this no more so than when it comes to production and project management. There are books a-plenty on commissioning, editing, design, and printing and binding, but nothing up to date on production management.

Although this makes it difficult to create a bibliography or reading list of any size, I have prepared a list of books for further reading that you may find useful:

Bann, David. *The All New Print Production Handbook*. RotoVision, 2006

Bennett, Roger. *Corporate Strategy and Business Planning*. Pitman Publishing, 2006

Burke, Rory. *Project Management Techniques*. Burke Publishing, 2007

Clark, Giles and Angus Phillips. *Inside Book Publishing*, 4th edition. Routledge, 2008

Dykes, Lucinda and Ed Tittel. *XML for Dummies*. Wiley, 2005

Graham, Nick and Stanley E. Portny. *Project Management for Dummies*, (UK edition). Wiley, 2011

Horn, Barbara. *Editorial Project Management*. Horn Editorial Books, 2006

Kasdorf, William (ed.). *The Columbia Guide to Digital Publishing*. Columbia University Press, 2003

Lee, Marshall. *Bookmaking, Editing, Design, Production*, 3rd edition. Norton, 2004

Maylor, Harvey. *Project Management*, 4th edition. Prentice Hall/Financial Times, 2010

Speirs, Hugh. *Print Estimator's Handbook*, 2nd edition. Pira International, 2005

# Index

Note: page numbers in **bold** refer to tables; page numbers in *italics* refer to figures.